CONTENTS

By the same Author:

Sai Baba, Man of Miracles
Sai Baba, Avatar
Walking the Path with Sai Baba
        (Also called *Sai Baba, Invitation to Glory)*
Where the Road Ends

Beyond Death, The Undiscovered Country
When Daylight Comes
Yankee Beacon of Buddhist Light
        (Also published as *Hammer on the Mountain*)
Yoga for Busy People

Front cover photos: Sathya Sai Baba and Howard Murphet
Back cover photo: Sai Baba with Iris and Howard Murphet

DEDICATION

This book is dedicated, with devotion and gratitude, to Bhagavan Sri Sathya Sai Baba who, from my first meeting with him in 1965 to the present year of 1995, has provided life-transforming experiences and insights, together with the inspiration to share these with others.

There is only one God and He is Omnipresent.

Sathya Sai Baba

PREAMBLE

Some experiences described or referred to in this book date back to a time before I had met, or even heard of, Sri Sathya Sai Baba. I now understand and accept the fact, from words he has spoken, that Sai Baba knew about my earlier movements and, when necessary, directed them and gave me protection long -- he alone knows how long -- before he appeared to me in the flesh as my guide and guru. For example, at times of great danger during World War II, I felt some hidden protection. Now I know where the protection came from.

During the months and years that have rolled past since my eyes first beheld his gracious human form, I know that he has watched over me with the loving care and solicitude of at least a million mothers. Every day I have felt it. Every day and night I feel it now.

The last time Iris and I visited our dearly loved Sathya Sai Baba together, early in the 1990's, he told us in private that as he was now securely in our hearts, as well as being all around us wherever we may be, there was really no need for us to suffer the austerities, discomforts, hardships and expense of travelling the distance from Australia to Puttaparthi, India, to see him. As I myself was then in my mid-eighties and my health suffered from long distance air travel -- not only during the journey but for several weeks afterwards -- I felt very grateful and relieved to hear those compassionate remarks from our Lord Sai. Iris, who was nearly seventeen years my junior, did not take so readily, I notice, to the idea of not seeing Baba again. I knew how she felt and I knew, too, that some kind of compromise on this matter lay ahead of us.

Any compromise would have been better than the one that actually took place. Before the question of the journey to India arose again, I sat by her bed of sickness and pain when she went out of her body into the waiting arms of Swami and thus into the realms of bliss where God is ever "nearer than hands and feet." Now, devastatingly alone, there was another reason why I should not make the journey to the ashram. Iris and I had spent so many heavenly times together there, it would be too painful for me to be there alone. In less than two months after my wife's passing away, however, I received an invitation from Swamiji to visit India to see him. My first reaction was that I did not want to go. But after two days, his message and invitation sank deep into my heart. It became the divine hook that pulled me strongly toward him. His formless omnipresence with me in Australia did not bring me what I now needed -- his physical presence, the look in his eyes, the touch of his hand and the sound of his voice. These were the divine comforts, the deep solace that I so much needed. Christmas, 1994, found me at Prashani Nilayam again. And Swami's physical presence did, indeed, bring me the comfort, peace and perspective I needed. There was an unexpected bonus, too. I had not made the journey with the intention, or even the hope, of gathering new material for this book, my fifth on the Avatar. But one cannot visit the spiritual center of the world with open mind and heart without gaining significant experiences and insights.

The best and most revealing of this windfall of Sai material was the story given me by a young doctor, Naresh Bhatia of Sai's renowned hospital near Prashanti Nilayam. I offer it gladly in the following pages.

1

WHO ARE YOU?

The questions of who you are and where you come from do not seem to present any great difficulty to the average citizen; but, in fact, they present a riddle that few people can answer. The answers go deeper than the name on your birth certificate and the address of your present residence or, indeed, any residence you have ever had on this earth. I remember, at a period when I was with Sai Baba in the 1960's, he went through a phase of asking people: "Who are you?" While I was present, only one person got the answer right. That was a Theosophist and Liberal Catholic priest by the name of Charles White. He said "I am I." "That's right," Swami said happily, but it was not the way Swami himself usually put the answer. On another day much later, after his schools were established at Prasanthi Nilayam, I heard him asking students from his primary school: "Where are you from?" Each confidently and proudly gave the address of his home in India. Finally one bright-eyed little boy of about six, standing in front of Swami with an expression of enthusiastic veneration on his face, gave the answer: "I am from you, Swami." Sai Baba gave him a pat on the head and sent him back to his seat; then he remarked to the gathering of boys before him, "He is the only one who got the answer right." Either the little fellow had an amazing perception of spiritual truths or his parents had trained him well. We may, of course, be taught by our parents, as many children are, that we are from God. We may, furthermore, be taught that Sai Baba is an Avatar of God or, more simply, that he is God on Earth in a human body, but this may not lead us to the answer Charles White gave to the question "Who are you?" That is -- "I am I."

To give that answer in prompt assurance, we must be aware that the "I" we use to identify ourselves refers to the true inner Self which is the God within each one of us. There is, however, a long road to this understanding from what we usually mean by the personal pronoun, when we say such things as: "I am young," or "I am old," or "I am rich," or "I am angry,"or "I am going on a visit to Russia."   In saying these things we refer to the little ego, the individual little self, moving around the world in a physical body. When we have made the journey from the little self to the great Self -- and understood mentally that the great Self, the great I, is in everybody and is, in fact, God -- we still have to realize the truth of it. We must experience it by some deep inner consciousness and know beyond any shadow of doubt that the days of the little self are over, that the strutting, selfish little ego was a character in a bad dream. He -- the one we had been identifying ourselves with -- was part of what is called the mortal dream. But now we are awake from that dream and are living a higher life in a world that is the same, yet very different. But to come to this wonderful, transcendental, life-changing experience, each one of us has to come to an acceptance of the truth through the rational mind. That is the first step which will eventually take us to the second step, leading to the leap across the gap from *samsara*, or the world of illusion, onto the shore of Truth, or Reality.

Unless you are a very exceptional person, born so close to the realization of the great transcendental truth that the touch of a master's hand can break the thin shell and bring you to your spiritual goal, you will, as I did, have to make the mental journey, perhaps long, perhaps short, along the road of the spiritual philosophies bequeathed to the world by the spiritual giants of the ages. To me, the most rational and acceptable was the one known as *Vedanta*, derived from the realizations by the great rishis of ancient India and backed by the Avatar of this age, Sri Sathya Sai Baba. By this I mean that the latter's teachings are the ancient Vedanta given in the modern idiom and impregnated with the divine love or prema so that they may well be called bhakti-Vedanta. Vedanta itself, as its name suggests, is derived from the Indian *vedas*, whose origins go back into the mists of time. Who can say when these Truth revelations of the *rishis* were first taught in their oral form?

Although the greatest and the best commentators on Vedanta may differ a little on certain aspects of its teachings, all agree that it reveals a fundamental truth about the origin and nature of the cosmos and of man himself. The number one truth they reveal is that there is only one God. Mankind has given Him many names throughout the centuries, but whatever He is called, there is only the one Being, without a second. This Being, whom I will call God, is the cause of all that exists. Back in the days when I was a worshipper of logic, I used to ask myself the question: "If God is the great cause of all, then what was the cause of God?" I found the answer in Vedanta: God, the one Being, the cause of all, had no cause because He is eternal with no beginning and no end. It is
understandable that the human mind at its present level of evolution cannot truly grasp such concepts as eternity and infinity or an infinite eternal Being such as God.

In some degree, however, we can understand and accept that idea of an eternal Being who is in some way or another the Father of all beings. It follows, therefore, that He is the Father of you and me and, since there was nothing else -- no other being or existence at the beginning of creation -- we must be of the same substance as the Father. The three great schools of Vedanta agree on this, but they don't agree on the reason why we appear to each other in different forms. Why is there this great diversity of forms appearing in the cosmos, yet derived from and in substance part of the One?

Putting the matter very simply, one school of Vedanta states that the multitude of forms in the cosmos do not exist at all. They are merely a great illusion, a dream in which we live. Perhaps this is what is called the mortal dream. It has been called the dream of prisoners, implying that we are all captives within the walls of illusion, or maya. When we wake from the dream and the great illusion is dispelled, we will realize that we are part of the One, that there never was, in truth, anything other than the one existence. This philosophic understanding is usually called Non-dualism. The answer to the question "Who are you?" , according to this understanding, is "I am God." Or, if you are a Hindu, "I am the Atman." Sai Baba accepted Charles White's answer "I am I," because I, the Self, is God or Atman.

The second school of Vedanta, known in English as qualified Non-dualism, likewise teaches that all separate souls are in reality part of the one divine being. But though an integral part of the one divine Being, of the One, from eternity, they have always been separate. We could perhaps say as an analogy that, though the pomegranate fruit is one, it is made up of many separate seeds within the skin of the one fruit. Another illustration is a mother hen is sitting with a large clutch of chickens under her feathers. We see her as one, and of course she is one, though at times she scatters in all directions! It is like creation when the many separate souls move out into the universe. At the end of the great dispensation, or *manvantara,* the souls come back to God, as the chickens after an hour of play may go back under the mother hen. In this qualified Non-dualism, there is still the illusion of the many, though the many are an integral part of the One, as the pomegranate seeds are an integral part of one fruit. But there is still only God, nothing but God, though we may in our ignorance look on the separate souls of individuals as if they were something other than God. So, according to this Vedantic understanding, the little boy spoke the truth when he said he was from Sai Baba, since he assumed that Sai Baba was God.

The third school of Vedanta, which is the one that most of the great religions of the West -- such as the Judaism and Christianity -- seem to follow, is that the one Being, Almighty God, Jehovah or Yahweh, created all things, the whole universe. Everything must have been created from Himself as nothing else was in existence. This is specially emphasized in the creation of man when the Old Testament states that God breathed into Adam, imbuing him with the Divine Spirit of his Maker. In this Vedantic teaching, all separate souls are made by God from His own Being. Therefore, as in the other branches of Vedantic teachings, we are all part of God and will remain through eternity part of Him, though always separate in form. In this understanding of Vedanta, the little chicks will never go back under the mother hen to form a oneness, but will forever stay around and near her, enjoying the bliss of her presence, derived from the knowledge and feeling of oneness.

To summarize the concept of the nature of man from the insights of Vedanta: In one picture, souls are never created separately but simply dream that they are separate. When they awake from the dream, they realize again their oneness with the Divine. In another picture, souls are eternally separate, yet not truly separate. They are the many within the One. The third picture shows them created as separate souls by God and from God's own substance. They will always remain separate in form though always fully aware of their oneness, their oneness with each other and with the Almighty Creator. The God residing at the center of each individual, constituting the true Self of that individual, is known to the Hindus as the *Atman*. This, in essence, is identical with the great Atma or the *Paramatma* which is the one Divine Creator or God. The true answer to Sai Baba's question to his various devotees, "Who are you?" was "I am the Atma." But he accepted the answer "I am I," knowing, no doubt, that the American Theosophist, Charles White, was aware that the I and the Atma are the same.

Through Vedanta, the higher mind, the rational mind, can lead us to this deepest understanding of our identity with our Divine Maker and hence to the understanding that we, like Him, are eternal beings -- beginningless and endless. We are part of the one life that pervades the universe. Therefore, in some form or another, we will live somewhere forever. But, though this glorious destiny of man can be known to us philosophically through the work of that great instrument, the higher mind, we cannot realize it and experience it until we take another step up the ladder of consciousness into what is known as the intuitional mind, which knows without the use of the thinking process at all. The great truths of existence which lie beyond the reach of the higher mind are known through this intuitional faculty, that is sometimes called the *buddhi*. Great scientists have sometimes reached it spontaneously through a doorway from the philosophical mind and find the solution to the mystery that is confronting them. Einstein was one of these, for example. Through meditation, this buddhi, or well of truth, might be reached briefly or for longer periods, but it will not be our permanent state until we reach Self-realization. Then, as St Paul said, we will see as we are seen and know as we are known, or words to that effect. So for the individual to truly know the answer to the question "Who am I?" he must take this upward leap in consciousness to where all things are new to him and he will find himself living a completely new life. Many people believe that a large number of individuals in the world will take this upward step in consciousness within the few years that lie ahead of us, and that the numbers so changed will constitute the "critical mass" that will change the whole of mankind. Thus the Golden Age will begin for humanity.

It is a great thing to know the purpose and goal of our journey. Look at it this way: the evolutionary journey of consciousness through earthly forms, from mineral through the vegetable kingdom, through the animal kingdom to the human level, took a very long time. Eons passed while that slow pilgrimage took place. But the journey has not stopped with man. In his earlier stages, man, like the lower forms of life before him, did not know the purpose of his life here. He was not aware that he was on an evolutionary journey. Therefore, he did not take any steps to help himself onward. His progress depended on outward forces and the passage of time. But now, as more and more people are becoming aware of the purpose, the meaning and the ultimate goal of life on earth, they can help themselves forward. They can change gear and move into a faster lane. Knowing that they are headed towards a place of peace and supreme happiness, they will naturally want to discover and make use of instruments that can speed them onwards. The great spiritual masters are ever close at hand and willing to give those instruments to all who are ready to receive them. Such great teachers constitute what is called the force-field of Light in the world today. There are many, many workers, high and lowly, in this great field of Light. Their aim is to bring consciousness, and therefore the life of mankind, to a higher and happier level. Those who work through spiritual disciplines towards their own self-development are among the workers in this field. I believe that at the head of it, leading the great army of Light against the obstructive forces of ignorance and darkness, is the Avatar of the age -- Sathya Sai Baba himself.

2

THE CROSS

I have heard world-renowned evangelists tell huge crowds that Christ was crucified to save all humanity. Then they state that unless a person accepts this teaching and follows the Christian way, he or she has no chance of reaching the highest abode of God, which they call Heaven. Although at times I have been thrilled by the earnest sincerity of speakers like Billy Graham, I can not accept the dogma that only people who believe Christ died for them have a chance to reach man's spiritual home with God. What about the millions who lived before Christ? Or the millions who lived in countries never reached by Christian teachings? The dogma of the fundamentalist Christian speakers seems very unjust indeed. But perhaps there is some symbolic, esoteric, meaning in this crucifixion story that is acceptable and enlightening to the modern mind.

I have heard Sai Baba give a symbolic meaning that sheds light on the mystery. He says that the crucifixion of Jesus symbolizes the death of everyman's little individual ego. The upright pole of the cross, he says, holding up one finger, represents man's ego; the crossbeam stands for its crossing out. The crossing out and final death of the ego are quite painful. A human life undergoes much suffering before the individual reaches the great climax -- the crucifixion of his/her ignorant ego. The sufferings provide the necessary steps up the hill of the Via Dolorosa to the hill of Calvary where the ego finally meets its death. Then, just as Jesus rose triumphant from the tomb, the higher, divine, true Self of man rises from the tomb of the body. This is known as self-realization. The event usually happens before the actual physical death of the body, but not before the death of the ego.

The Christ-story teaches that Jesus ascended to the Father; similarly, when the human individual rises to his divine Self, he becomes merged with the one God of the universe -- the one

Jesus called the Father. A Christian hymn expresses it: "I lie in dust, life's glory dead, /And from the ground there blossoms red, /Life that will endless be."

This is an illuminating explanation of the symbolic meaning of the crucifixion story. We must all walk the narrow, suffering way -- the Via Dolorosa of our lives -- to reach the glorious culmination, our final mergence with God. But did one pure, innocent man have to endure the indescribable sufferings of the first Good Friday in order to teach us the most important lesson about the meaning of human life -- the reason each of us is here on earth? Couldn't the same thing have been accomplished symbolically or ceremonially, as demonstrated in the ancient temples of Egypt? There, when an individual was ready for this initiation, he was stretched on a cross, lying on the floor of the temple. Then he left his physical body, travelling into the lower regions of the astral plane, the netherworld where he taught the great truths of life to the suffering souls. On the third day, he returned to his body, still stretched on the cross in the temple, as an enlightened or self-realized man. The meaning of the ancient Egyptian ritual was revealed only to the few ready for the lesson.

How many ages would have passed before mankind learned the truth in this way? The ritual had to be put into actuality by the suffering and agonizing death of one innocent man. This mighty world drama revealed the divine love of the enlightened Son of God. For the many suffering sons of God who were walking in darkness, the impact of this momentous event on the human mind was so great that it went into the world and formed the foundation of a great new religion -- the religion that revealed the reality of divine love and showed the meaning and value of human suffering. Surely this unforgettable lesson -- revealing that the ego must die before an individual can reach oneness with God and, further, that divine love alone can bring about this unity -- is meant for all mankind.

A valuable, esoteric lesson also lies in the crucifixion story. Centuries ago, the priest-poet, John Donne, proclaimed a deep truth: that no man is an island; that beneath the waters of appearances (called *maya* by the Hindus), all individual souls belong to the same continent.   This is also true of the geographical islands; all are one beneath the ocean.   Because of the fundamental oneness in man, each individual's behavior affects all mankind.   In other words, there is karma, not only for an individual, but for humanity as a whole.   The karma of humanity can sink; indeed, many times in the history of mankind, it has sunk to a very low level.

No doubt one of the all-time "lows" existed in the dark days of the Roman Empire, particularly in what we now call the Western World.   One of the greatest spiritual teachers of our day, Rudolf Steiner, revealed through his esoteric vision, that the individual dark egos of that period in time were reaching a power. If the power had continued to increase, the divine plan for the evolution of human consciousness would have been upset.   The tug of war between good and evil, necessary for that evolution, was moving dangerously over the line into the hands of the destructive forces of evil.   This could have meant the final conquest of evil over good, which the old Norse mythology taught was the ultimate fate of mankind.

The spiritual Masters, however -- like the founders of all the great religions -- teach that the Divine Plan is for the ultimate victory of Light over darkness, of good over evil.   So it was that at the beginning of our Christian era, from which the measurement of modern time begins, God himself took a hand to right the balance.   He walked the earth in the body of Jesus of Nazareth, as today he walks the earth in the body of Sathya Sai Baba.

Christian theologians have decided that Jesus was the Son of God, yet Jesus himself proclaimed that He and the Father were one.   Therefore the Son is the Father and the Father the Son. There is no difference.   Are we not able to say, then, in deepest truth: That it was the one God of the universe who walked the Via Dolorosa to Calvary on the terrible, yet glorious, Friday before the first Easter?   That it was He, Himself, who taught the crucial lesson to every individual?   That the only road to God, our divine destination, is the narrow road of suffering to the mount of the ultimate agony where the ego is crucified?

Surely, God Himself taught the other great lesson of the cross. He told His close followers that the way to salvation, which He had demonstrated -- the way of suffering, eased and blessed by the love of God for man -- leads to the crowning glory when the selfish little individual self is sacrificed to the unity, the eternal, blissful unity between God and man.

This gospel, this glad news, was spread to the nations of the earth by the courageous apostles St. Paul, St. Joseph of Arimathea and many others. They met fearsome and bloody resistance from the powerful egos of the time. The primary ones were the Roman emperors and their legions. Finally, after the martyrdom of hundreds of apostles and the death of many thousands in the armies of Christ, the religion of the new, enlightened human values was victorious. Jesus replaced Zeus; men throughout Christendom strove to live by higher and more enlightened ideals. Did it not benefit all mankind for the new light to shine in the world, a result of the crucifixion of Christ? Much evil remained -- and remains still -- but the balance was righted in the tug of war between angels and demons, Light and Dark, good and evil.

Why the tug of war? According to the Hindu myth, it takes place in the ocean of milk, the veil of illusory appearances in which we live our earthly lives. As in milk there is butter hidden that must be churned out, so within the false appearances, within which we live our lives of the senses, spiritual reality is hidden. It, likewise, must be churned out. As the two sides of the tug of war move backward and forward, they move a churning stick that brings good things out of the ocean of milk. Similarly, the back and forth swaying of good and evil, pain and pleasure, desires and controls in our human lives churn out the divine development in our consciousness, thus in our natures. The great struggle between good and evil must go on until every individual in the human race is divinised. Then, earthly matter will be divinised and the Kingdom of Heaven will come to earth. Until then, the churning must continue and it can only do so if the opposing sides are kept in the right balance by the hand of God. If the balance is seriously endangered, the Divine One Himself takes a hand. Two thousand years ago, He did that through the man Jesus.

The crucifixion story symbolically shows the road each of us must take to reach the spiritual goal of our human journey. Looked at through esoteric spectacles, we can see its great historic value, halting the downward slide of mankind and turning our human pilgrimage again toward the Light. Looked at in this way, there is no doubt that Jesus, the Christ, shared his blood on Calvary for the benefit of all mankind.

But is something more to be considered surrounding the mighty event that changed mankind's history and set a new time scale for all nations? Why do the sermons and hymns of Christians make so much of the blood shed on Calvary? Why do they emphasize that the blood of Christ was shed for us? Is the blood just a symbol of the actual sacrifice He made, or is there other significance? Some great teachers of the occult give a reason, a teaching that may not be easily accepted by the skeptical, down-to-earth minds of today. Though we may not readily accept it, we should not too easily toss it aside as unworthy of our consideration. Remember that some of the great truths we accept today were scoffed at ten or more years ago. We need to keep our minds open toward the tireless teacher, Time.

In brief, the occult teaching -- particularly from Rudolf Steiner -- is this: the blood of the innocent, divine man, Christ, dripped to the earth from the wounds made by nails and the crown of thorns, the wounds made by the scourging, and especially from the thrust into his side from the spear, made by the Roman legionnaire, Longinus. It acted like a trace element, bringing Christ's spirit into Mother Earth. Thus the Earth was imbued with the Cosmic Christ. Even the skeptical, scientific mind of today is beginning to understand that Mother Earth is not just a ball of dead matter but is, in fact, a living and breathing entity.

More and more people now realize that the earth is a living being and that the actions of mankind affect the reactions of the earth. As the following story demonstrates, Sai Baba makes this clear.

One night, I received a long distance call from Copenhagen. The caller's name was Steen Piculell. He phoned to say that he had been made Deputy Coordinator for all Russian-speaking countries; then he explained the reason behind the appointment. Steen had gone into a book shop in Copenhagen and asked for a spiritual book to read on a holiday to the Canary Islands. The shop assistant offered him the Danish translation of my book, *Sai Baba Avatar*. He looked dubious, but the woman said it was the best spiritual book she had, so Steen bought it. A few weeks later he lay on the beach on the Canary Islands reading the book. "I read it right through," Steen told me. "Then I felt as if a bolt of lightening had gone through me. I knew for sure that God was on earth. That evening I went for a walk on the beach to think about the revelation from the book. Then Sai Baba began to talk to me. Among other things, he said, "The earth is a living being. It breathes. At the present time it is breathing bad air into the universe, which is also a living being. The bad air is coming from Europe. I have to change that. There are many people helping me in this work and you will be one of them." Steen went on to tell me that, not surprisingly, this experience had taken him quickly to Prasanthi Nilayam in India and led eventually to his being given this special job.

Could it be, then, that our beloved Earthly Mother, to whom we are so callous and inconsiderate today, received a revitalizing, rejuvenating essence from the blood of the Godman who carried the spirit and power of the Earth's great Creator? Mother Earth has stood a lot from her children in two thousand years, particularly in recent decades. Perhaps she could do with another stimulating shot in the arm. But at least let us have compassion and consideration for her suffering.

3

A LIGHT FROM REBIRTH AND KARMA

A Jewish rabbi wrote a very readable book, *Why Do Bad Things Happen To Good People?* Many people have pondered this question and the related one: "Why do good things happen to bad people?" The rabbi could find no answer to these questions in theology or philosophy. Nor, I suspect, can the majority of Christian ministers. The only satisfactory answer, I think, lies in the doctrines of rebirth -- reincarnation and karma. These doctrines were taught as truths by such eminent ancient philosophers as Plato, the ancient enlightened rishis of India and the great Buddha. Strangely, Christ Himself did not propound such teachings, though he seemed to have accepted the truth of rebirth, current in Palestine during his life. This fact is shown in a number of episodes of the New Testament. For instance, when His disciples remarked that people thought Jesus was a reincarnation of Elijah, Jesus told them that Elijah had already come and had been killed by the ignorant people of the time. The disciples knew he was speaking of John the Baptist. In another episode, Jesus cured a man who had been born blind. His disciples asked if the blindness had resulted from the man's own sin or that of his parents. It could only have been the result of his own sin had he lived a former life. Jesus did not rebuke his disciples for asking the question, which implied rebirth of the soul; surely he would have done so if the doctrine had been untrue. Either Jesus had some good reason of His own for not teaching the gospel of rebirth, or else what He said on the subject has not been included in the writings of the New Testament. Records show that the early Christian church included this doctrine in their teaching. Yet I can find no evidence that it played a substantial part in the gospels of the early apostles, in the early days in Britain or later, in Rome. After several centuries of church history, Roman Catholic leaders banned the teaching. Yet some popes continued to believe in it.

Many eminent philosophers, scholars and poets of the Western world have accepted reincarnation of the human soul through many lifetimes as the only just explanation for why some good people suffer pain and tragedy in their lives and some bad people prosper.

Let us take a closer look at this ancient teaching. It sheds light on some otherwise inexplicable happenings in our lives, on the divine destiny that shapes our lives -- often in spite of our own efforts -- and on the ultimate goal of human life.

The doctrine has been accepted by millions of people through many centuries. It is reflected in the old bible dictum, "As you sow, so shall you also reap," but it becomes clearer when spread out over a broad span of time, so that our sowing may take place in one lifetime and the harvest reaped in another. The Sanskrit word, karma, means "action," but we tend to think of it in terms of the *results* of our actions. While many results are quite obvious in a physical sense -- such as building a house, making a road or writing a book -- there are also hidden results that have a great deal to do with our motives in the action. If the motive is entirely self-centered, with no consideration for the effects of the outcome on other people, then the hidden results will be bad and will rebound on the doer -- either on the development of his character in this lifetime, or in unhappy results later in this lifetime or in a future life. If a philanthropist does good deeds with the pure motive of bringing happiness and benefit to others, there will also be a harvest of happiness and prosperity to the philanthropist, either in this life or in lives to come.

Many students of this great spiritual doctrine may think, as I used to, that the weakness lies in the gap between the sowing and the reaping of the harvest. We do not even remember the past bad seeds we sowed. It is as if some other person sowed them, for there is no memory-connection between the present life and past ones. Would it not be better, they ask, if we remembered our past evil deeds and therefore knew why we are suffering today? Perhaps it would help, but perhaps not. I, for example, have suffered near-blindness, through hemorrhages in both eyes, for a number of years. I believe that the condition is karma and that I must learn some lesson through suffering. A friend, who is able to see into past lives, told me of my misdeeds centuries ago. The information included my name at that time and the nature of my bad actions, motivated by vengeance.   But my friend did not throw any light on what I already accepted in a general way. I knew I was undergoing karmic suffering and that the challenge before me was to accept and learn from such suffering.

I know that I have lived several lifetimes on earth since that long-ago century when the Christian knights drove the Moorish armies back from the borders of France. According to my seer friend, it was then that I sowed the seeds for my present terrible eye trouble. So the harvest of weeds may take a long time to sprout, to grow and mature. Bad seeds may give their harvest in this present lifetime or many lifetimes hence.

The ancient wisdom, known as the *sanathana dharma*, teaches that before each of our incarnations on earth, a decision is made by our Higher Selves -- or by the divine functionaries, the Lords of Karma -- about which particular portion of our big stock of accumulated karma will be dealt with in the lifetime about to begin.   So we come to earth bearing our selected bundle of karma. The great bard saw this truth when he wrote the lines "There is a Divinity that shapes our ends, rough hew them as we will." Ultimately, the Divinity shapes through His divine agents as part of His plan for our evolution in the university of adversity, which we call earth.

People often think of karma as "an eye for an eye, a tooth for a tooth" punishment.   But karma is not the operation of a mechanical law or a punishment imposed on us from without, but the effect of the soul's craving for balance and healing. If a person has been responsible for evil, the soul accepts the need for the individual to undergo suffering in order to experience the suffering he has caused others; thus, he can accept responsibility for this suffering with a full and deep awareness -- a lived awareness. Such experience and acceptance will enable him to achieve the balance and wholeness he lost when he caused harm to others. Our task is to let go of our attachment to evil, to forgive and forget where we have suffered and, where we have erred, to forgive ourselves and to seek forgiveness from and make reparation to those we have harmed. Toward the end of this growth process, we begin to live our lives so that we do unto others as we would have them do unto us.

An important point in the spiritual philosophy of rebirth and karma is that during our present lives we are -- with our thoughts, words and deeds -- adding to the great pile of karma in the invisible planes. The warehouse of karma is waiting for us to work through and learn lessons in future lifetimes. It seems like a vicious cycle of cause and effect ruling our human destinies and, perhaps, continuing through eternity. Is there no way to break the turning wheel of karma?

Yes, there is a sure and certain way that I will come to in a moment. First, let us consider the Christian teaching of forgiveness of sins. When dealing with a disease he knew resulted from sin, Jesus said, "Your sins are forgiven. Go your way and sin no more." That was the perfect formula -- provided the patient sinned no more and made no more karmic errors. A very unlikely thing. Sathya Sai Baba has been known to say to groups of people, for reasons that only he himself knows, "Your karma to this point has been wiped out." But soon, if not immediately afterwards, they begin creating new karma for themselves. What is the way to prevent this and smash asunder the wheel of karma? The answer has to do with motivation. We cannot avoid action in this life because words, and even thoughts, create our future karma. If our thoughts and words are evil, violent or against our fellow men, our harvest of karma will be bad. Even if more benign, our words, thoughts and deeds may serve to seal us into attachment to the things of earth. What should the motivating force behind all our actions be? The laws of karma yoga, as expounded daily by Sathya Sai Baba, are simple and easy to learn, but they require a great deal of constant practice to put into effect. They are this: we should not grasp for the fruits of our actions, but offer all fruits to God. Put in another way, all that we think, say or do must have the aim of serving the Divine One. We may see the Divine One in our fellow men, in all creatures of God's creation or in the Transcendent One whose great plan we strive to understand and help to promote. To whatever extent we can remove the target of our action from our own interests to the welfare of God's creation, that is the extent to which we can finally break the wheel of karma that we ourselves have created. The *yogic* discipline, aided by the love and grace of God, is the only sure way off the painful grinding wheel of karmic cause and effect that rules our lives.

Sai Baba makes a revealing point: a Godman or Avatar will not interfere in a person's karma if in so doing he would slow down or handicap the person's spiritual progress. Therefore, when any Godman says "Your sins are forgiven," or "Your karma has been removed," it means that the person concerned has already learned the lessons that the karma was destined to teach. In other words, his karma is nearing its end and the remainder of it can be remitted. Otherwise, any karma lifted by the Godman will have to be suffered in a future life.

An incident in my early days at the ashram illustrates this. A young teen-aged woman suffered from a bad disfigurement of the skin which she had been born with. When the other girls at school laughed and teased her about the ugliness of her skin, the young woman suffered great pain. The parents, close to Sai Baba, asked him if he would use his divine power to remove the disfigurement and make life happier for their daughter. Swami considered the request for quite a while. In the end he said to them, "I can remove it, and will do so if you wish. But remember that it is karmic; if she doesn't suffer it in this life, she will have to in the next. Is it not better for her to go through it now while she has kind parents and my grace to help her, because I will make the burden easier for her to bear. It is better for her to have the karmic lesson in this life rather than the next, but I leave it for you to decide." The parents decided it was wiser to follow Swami's advice and let her learn her karmic lesson now, rather than defer it to the unknown circumstances and conditions of the next life. Swami probably knew that they would make the compassionate decision, but he had to let them make it to earn good karma for themselves.

We should attempt to consider this question: Is there such a thing as group karma, national karma and the karma of humanity? It seems to me that if we accept the truth that beneath surface appearances we are all one, then it follows that the thoughts, words and deeds of every individual in the group, be it small, medium or large, must have an effect for good or evil to some extent on the life and destiny of the group. It follows, then, that as we help to create the karma of the group, we must be affected by it.

Take my own particular case as an example. When I landed in England in July, 1939, I had great plans for the promotion of my own individual career. But those plans for self-promotion and individual self-interest were swept away like chaff before the wind as the great karmic hurricane of mankind, World War II, hit my life and millions of others in September, 1939. It brought about what appeared to be a grand-scale change of destiny through the cyclonic winds of mankind's group karma. Yet, viewed through the long perspective of time, I see that this sweeping change was an instrument to help promote my own divine destiny. In other words, my individual, personal karma had its own intricate course within the karmic pattern of the war. The experiences, insights and even the horrors of the war-time world were part of the divine destiny driving me toward the work I was destined to do for God. Despite my many faults, my hands are still on the plough that turns my destined furrow in the fields of God.

No doubt the doctrine of reincarnation explains many of life's problems -- not only that which troubled the worthy rabbi.

Perhaps it explains: the greatly differing talents and gifts people are born with, from genius to moron; the fatal diseases with which some people are born, making their lives very short; the reason some people are born with a warped and criminal tendency in the mind while others seem angelic from birth. These and many others of life's puzzles are explicable on the basis of multiple lifetimes for one individual. While the average citizen may spend long periods, even centuries, between lifetimes on earth, there are others, like those who die in childhood and advanced yogis who want to deal quickly with the remaining part of their soul's necessary pilgrimage, who are reborn quickly.

There is an interesting story of an old yogi who was about to shed his body on a river bank in Northern India. He asked a wandering *sadhu* to dispose of his remains, giving him the exact amount of money required for this purpose. He told the sadhu that he had only one more life to live before reaching his liberation and that he was going to be reborn straight after his passing to the wife of a blacksmith who lived on the outskirts of Calcutta. He said he would be born a girl in the next incarnation, would live a very quiet, contemplative life in the village of the blacksmith and leave the body at the age of sixteen. He even favored the sadhu with the name and address of the blacksmith. The sadhu made several visits to the blacksmith, finding that a baby girl was born to his wife less than a year after the old yogi's death. Later visits revealed that the girl lived quietly, spending most of her time in the temple or in meditation. The old yogi's foreknowledge of his coming life proved to be correct, but why he had to live this short life as a quiet village girl, spending her time in devotion to God, is, of course, a mystery. Indeed, reflection and contemplation on this penetrating doctrine reveal that while it explains so many human problems, much of it remains a great mystery.

There is also the problem that acceptance of the doctrine of karma may lead to self-indulgent procrastination. I have heard people in India say, for example, "Yes, I must do this or that but

I will leave it to my next lifetime." An even worse attitude is that of not helping people in dire distress or danger because such action would interfere with the person's karma. If, for example, a person is drowning, a negative attitude to the laws of karma may lead the onlooker to say "I must not attempt to save his life because that would be interfering with his karma." Such a negative understanding of karma may deter someone from attempting to heal a sick person. Though this negative, reverse-gearing exists, it is fortunately not very prevalent. Of course, if a patient's karma is to die, your help will not save his life, but by failing to attempt to help the victim of disease or misfortune, you build bad karma for yourself. By doing your utmost to help and save the victim of disease or circumstance, you are creating good personal karma.

Is it possible that the danger of such negative thinking is the reason the doctrines of rebirth and karma are not taught in the Western religions of Islam and Christianity? Perhaps the aim of the great founders of these religions was to create a culture in which individuals believe they have only one life on earth, making them work urgently to achieve what they feel must be done without procrastination. In this way, they develop a more active compassion. It does seem that compassionate welfare work is more prevalent and progressive in the West than in the East. Moreover, the lifestyle of the West has a greater speed and urgency, as if there is hardly a minute to live; in the East, life moves in a more leisurely way, as if time is its servant rather than its master. Yet it seems doubtful that this is the reason. For it is not strong enough to justify leaving so many people in dark ignorance of a great truth which throws so much light on the purpose, progress, evolutionary development and ultimate destination of mankind's pilgrimage on earth. Whatever the reason for the ignorance about this important teaching among the masses of the Western world, it is heartening to know that Avatar Sai Baba is now spreading the word, revealing teachings of rebirth and karma to every country. It will be integral to the higher spiritual philosophy of the approaching Golden Age.

4

STEPPING ACROSS THE WORLD

God without form vibrates in every atom of the Universe. As the Holy Spirit, he is therefore omnipresent. Why then does he need to travel, to step across the universe anywhere from pole to pole in his form in order to carry out some particular mission of mercy or faith? If he had been able to do the same work without a body after he left his Shirdi form, and remained in close touch with the earth, he would not have taken his present body at Puttaparthi. Perhaps this gives some indication as to why, when he wants to do a particular job at any spot on the globe, he goes there in a subtle form -- usually, but not always, a replica of his present *Avataric* form we know as Sathya Sai Baba. Human beings at the spot do not always see his subtle form, because the clairvoyance of most of us is not sufficiently developed. But many who do not see, or even hear, the subtle presence may feel it powerfully, though indescribably, as what the ancient Romans called the numina or the numinous.

My late friend, the American spiritual millionaire, Walter Cowan, was one of those able to see the form of Sai Baba, yet his wife Elsie, who was just as devoted as Walter, was unable to see him in the ordinary way, though she could always feel the divine presence. Once long ago, in the late 1960's, when the Cowans and my wife and I were staying in Bangalore at different addresses and traveling daily to Brindavan to spend the time with Sathya Sai Baba, both Walter and I fell ill. At the time Sai Baba had gone away to Madras for two or three days. I don't remember what ailed Walter, nor do I know what was wrong with me. I only know that I felt very ill. I went to bed and sent for a medical doctor, but he could not diagnose my sickness. My friend Walter was also bed-ridden; indications were that both of us were in for a prolonged period of illness. Since we expected Swami back in a day or two, we did not want him to find us laid up in bed, so the four of us, in constant touch by telephone, decided to pray to Sai

Baba to bring a quick healing to Walter and me. Next morning, I woke up completely normal. Iris phoned Elsie who said Walter was also completely well. She said Swami came in the night and cured him. "I did not see him, but I felt his presence and heard him. Walter saw him quite clearly; I wish I could. I did ask him to go over and cure Howard. He replied that he had already been there and that Howard was not well." I have no doubt that Swami could have healed us from the house where he was staying two hundred miles away in Madras, but for some reason of his own, he chose to visit us in his subtle body. Whether this so-called subtle body is what occultists call the astral body, or something else, I do not know. I only know that Swami is able to solidify it into earthly matter so it can be felt by the human sense of touch. Furthermore, there is evidence that more than one Sai subtle body can be operating in different places at the same time. It has been seen by the human extrasensory perception in some very unexpected places.

Princess Nanda of Kutch, who was living at Swami's ashram during the 60's when we were there, told us that a friend of hers had been a passenger on a plane which crashed somewhere in the Arctic circle, not far from the North Pole. The friend had been knocked unconscious in the crash. When she regained consciousness, she opened her eyes and saw that many dead and wounded passengers were scattered about her. She saw only one figure moving about -- one she was sure had not been on the plane. He was such an unusual figure, dressed in a red-orange robe and with a mop of fuzzy hair. Surely, she would have noticed him had he been among the passengers on the journey. Now he moved about from body to body on the ground. Soon she went off into another faint and, returning later to consciousness, the strange, small figure in the red-orange robe had vanished.

I cannot remember the details of her rescue; the point Princess Nanda wanted to make was that months later, when her friend saw a photograph of Sai Baba, she was greatly surprised. "That is the man I saw walking among the dead and wounded passengers after the plane crashed in the polar regions," she exclaimed. I have no doubt that Swami had gone to the scene in his subtle body in order to bring immediate help to those still living and guidance to the spirits of those who had met a violent death. Such is his compassion to all people.

Whether the woman who saw him was normally clairvoyant, or whether the shock of the accident had stimulated her clairvoyant faculty -- as is known to happen -- I cannot say. It is of interest that psychic and para-psychological researches have shown that normal human beings have some degree of clairvoyance. This extrasensory faculty, which is apparent in many forms of animal life, seems to have been buried in a kind of hibernation under modern man's intensive intellectual development. It does, however, awake briefly under certain conditions and at certain times. One of the circumstances is physical or
mental shock; one of the times is that brief period between sleep-consciousness and wide-awake consciousness.

The remarkable clairvoyant, Joan Moylan, for example, told me that she had been an ordinary practicing psychologist before an accident awoke her clairvoyant faculty which, fortunately for many people, has continued to be active and even seems to have increased in power. The transitional period of clairvoyance -- that is, the gap between sleeping and waking -- is something I have experienced myself. It has to do with the story I am about to relate: of how Sai Baba stepped across some five thousand miles of the earth's surface from his ashram in India to Adelaide, South Australia -- thereby saving my life.

In the winter of 1982, my wife, Iris, and I had rented a friend's house for a few months in the Adelaide Hills, just outside the city at a place called Aldgate. While there, my symptoms of swollen prostate gland got worse, so I consulted a specialist recommended by a doctor friend of ours. The urologist urged me to have an operation without delay. I agreed, but did not improve my popularity with the doctor because I elected to go into a big public hospital instead of the private one he recommended. I heard that he had some financial interest in that small private hospital. He did agree, somewhat reluctantly, to perform the surgery in the public hospital of my choice. In his consulting rooms, he said symptoms indicated there were probably warts in my bladder and that during the prostate operation he would look into that, as some of the warts might be malignant.

The operation did not go well at all. When I was returned from the operating theater into the recovery room, my wife asked the urologist if he had looked into the bladder as promised. She found that he had completely forgotten that part of the surgery. With some truculence, he ordered me back into the theater on the same day. When I regained consciousness in the recovery room after the second operation, I realized that there was a state of alarm. I was hemorrhaging badly. Eventually I had to be given a blood transfusion.

After spending more than the normal time in the hospital for recovery from prostate surgery, I finally found myself in our camper-van with Iris on the half-hour journey home to Aldgate in the Hills. Happy I was to get there, but during the ensuing days, because symptoms showed that all was not well, I had to go several times to Adelaide for medical tests. The urologist who had botched my operation had gone abroad, reporting that he was required to give specialist advice to urological departments in some foreign country. Eventually, I began to wonder if he was dodging responsibility for things he had done to me. I was handed over to one of his colleagues in Adelaide who did not tell me the shattering news: I had contracted Golden Staph, hospital variety (Staphylococcus). I later learned there are several varieties of this disease; the worst one is known as the hospital variety because there are only two antibiotics that have a chance of curing it. If they don't work, it is incurable -- and fatal.

The doctor who was treating me in Adelaide administered a course of the first antibiotic in the form of tablets without telling me what it was for. When after a few days I broke out with blotches all over my skin, he finally told me the disease I was suffering from. He said since the first treatment had failed, I would have to take the second possible cure, but for that, I would have to return to hospital.

This alarmed me and I asked if my wife, a trained, long-experienced nurse, could give me the treatment at home. Unfortunately, that was not possible, he said, because it was a very powerful drug and had to be administered by special equipment which injected it at prescribed intervals into the veins. The hospital agreed, somewhat reluctantly we thought, to admit me again on the following day.

I understood their reluctance when I learned from Iris that this form of Golden Staph, contracted in hospitals through what she called "dirty surgery," had been known to spread so quickly and pervasively through patient populations that hospitals had to close down, evacuating all patients until the unpopular invader had been completely cleared out. How long that took I do not know. But when I arrived at the hospital the following day, I was not surprised to see concerned and worried faces on the nurses and the doctors.

I was put in a two-bed ward, but the man already there was hustled out rather quickly. I was told I must stay in this room, which was for me alone, and must use no other facilities in the hospital. Also, I was to have no visitors except my wife. Altogether, I began to feel like a leper. Two doctors immediately began to erect some equipment over my bed, through which they would give me the intravenous injections. I was to have several of these injections each day for about five days. They warned there could be some side-effects, such as loss of vitality and reduced hearing ability. I prayed to my *sadguru*, Sai Baba, to shield me against such bad side-effects. At the end of the treatment, my hearing did not seem to be any worse than usual, but I felt so weak that I could not stand. Tests showed that the disease had either been cured or put in remission, but I must have further tests after a few days before they could declare me cured.

In the meantime, I could go home. As I was unable to walk, they put me in a wheelchair and took me to our camper-van, where Iris had set up the bed ready for me. I lay down and she drove me out of Adelaide and up into the Hills to our temporary home in Aldgate.

I was overjoyed to be there and spent the remainder of the day resting in the tranquil, silent atmosphere of the country setting. But the next morning, symptoms began to reappear. Iris phoned the hospital, as she had been instructed to do, and told them of my condition. The doctors said I must come back to the hospital immediately. I did not want to go. In fact, I felt that if I went back and had to go through another course of the debilitating intravenous injections, I would not come out of the hospital alive. Yet, as the Golden Staph was still active, my only chance of survival was probably to return for further treatment. As I felt I could not go that day, I asked Iris to say I would return to the hospital the next morning. The doctors reluctantly agreed, but asked Iris to monitor my wildly jumping temperature and keep an eye on the other symptoms. She was instructed to report to them if things got worse. She promised to do so.

I felt unable to eat any lunch, so I lay down on the long leaf-green couch in the lounge room, where large windows opened onto the countryside all around. With the autumn sun streaming through the window, it seemed like a room in paradise. For a while, we prayed together for a miraculous cure for this terrible disease. When Iris left me alone in the room, I continued to pray more fervently, more intensely, than I had done before, then I drifted off to sleep. When I awoke, perhaps an hour later, Sai Baba was standing beside my bed with his hand circling above me in a gesture I had known so well during my years in India -- the gesture that seems to concentrate his divine power for the execution of supernormal phenomena. My moment of clairvoyance did not last long. First the form faded, leaving only the hand circling above me, and soon that faded from my vision, too. But I knew that my Lord Sai was still there because the whole room was filled with the inexplicable feeling of his divine presence. The feeling is one of uplifting joy and deep reverence, plus something else beyond words. It is generally called the numinous, or perhaps the numina, the words used by the ancient Romans when they felt the presence of their gods from on high whom they had not pictured in any form. This was probably before they took for themselves the Greek gods of Olympus, changing the names but keeping the Greek forms.

When Sai Baba comes in form with great power, even those who cannot see him can sometimes feel the numinous in his presence. On this occasion, I both saw and felt. Psychic science has proved that everybody has a degree of clairvoyance buried deep within, and that short period of consciousness between sleeping and waking is the time when it will probably become active. Perhaps that is why I was blessed briefly with a sight of my beloved Swami standing beside my couch.

When at last the wonderful feeling in the room faded and I felt that Swami had gone, I arose from the couch, stretched myself, and knew for certain that I had been cured. Then I went through a door into a smaller room where my wife had been sitting while I slept. She was not surprised when I told her of my wonderful experience, because she, too, had felt the numinous of Swami's presence through the wall, though she had not seen him. Her face was radiant with joy and she knew Swami's blessed visit with divine power to our house in the Adelaide Hills had healed me of a killing disease.

We both went down on our knees to offer our humble thanks to him. The hospital doctors probably thought they had cured me after all, but did not send me a bill for the second visit to the hospital -- showing that they accepted responsibility for the Golden Staph infection.

Now, some twelve years later, looking back on the Adelaide experience through the perspective of time, I see that Swami's visit did more than save my life. Each move he makes seems to achieve several things in the furtherance of his divine work and mission. On the Sunday after my miraculous cure, two visitors appeared at our Aldgate house. They were Indians by the name of Sri K. Soman and Dr. Vitty. I think they had both been to India to see Sathya Sai Baba some time before this visit. They stayed to talk for a while, then asked respectfully if they could bring two or three more people on the following Sunday. As this was obviously Sai work, we agreed and each weekend the numbers increased until many car-loads arrived each Sunday afternoon and the large lounge room, with its leaf-green furniture and wide windows looking out over the rolling countryside, was filled with people eager to hear about Sai Baba. Some of them were students of Vedanta; some had read a book or two on Sai Baba; all had heard about him and wanted to know more. Perhaps the enchanted room where Swami had appeared to me was an inspiration to us all. At any rate, the feeling of joy and devotion increased as the group learned to sing bhajans, guided by Iris and some learning tapes we had, and I talked to them about Sai Baba's teachings and our personal experiences with him in India.

Thus, during the winter of 1982, at the house in Aldgate in the Adelaide Hills, the foundations for the Sai movement in South Australia were laid.

5

LIVING STONES

Mystics affirm that the mineral kingdom has consciousness, but it is a sleeping consciousness. If that be so, then there are stones that walk in their sleep. As the Cross is a symbol of sacrifice to Christians, so the oval-shaped stone is a symbol of creation to the Hindus, but it belongs to the class of symbols that has an inherent power in themselves, as well as representing something sacred or spiritual. The Cross is believed by many to have a similar inherent power. As the spear of destiny thrust into the side of Jesus on Calvary is said to have a power of good or evil in the destiny of mankind, so the oval-shaped *lingam* can have the power for good or evil in the destiny of an individual. Whether its influence is beneficent or malevolent depends on its treatment by its owner.

Lingams can vary in size from less than an inch in length to the hundred-foot one with which, according to Hindu mythology, a powerful demon wreaked havoc on Earth. Finally, to save the Earth, the warrior son of Lord Siva, known as Scanda, or Subramanyam, did battle with the demon, overcame him and broke up the lingam into many pieces. Most of the pieces, all several feet in length, fell into India from the scene of the battle. According to the story, one fell at Mecca in Arabia and is the great stone worshipped by the Moslems. Perhaps the Moslems do not agree that this was the origin of their sacred stone. The large lingams that landed in India had temples built around them; temple priests perform sacred rituals to the lingams so their power will be auspicious and of benefit to mankind. With this power of destruction and reconstruction attributed to them, it is appropriate that the lingam should be especially sacred to Lord Siva, the compassionate god who destroys old, outworn forms and customs and replaces them with the new. He is the regenerating facet of the one God who creates, maintains and destroys when necessary. As Tennyson says, "God fulfils himself in many ways, lest one good custom should corrupt the world."

There is no doubt that the lingams of stone or metal that used to form inside the body of Sri Sathya Sai Baba -- to be ejected through his mouth on *Sivarathri* Day -- had this double-edged power. The old Rajah of Venkatagiri told me during my early days in India that at one Sivarathri festival, Sai Baba gave him a lingam that had sprung from the *Avatar*'s mouth. Swami knew that the Rajah would perform the regular, strict rituals that would keep the symbol's power auspicious. Swamiji always gives them to an appropriate person, Rajah told me, and if no such person is available, he sends them back to the Unmanifest from where they came. But the following story suggests that Sathya Sai Baba sometimes takes a risk and, if the recipient of the lingam fails to carry out, strictly, the demanding rituals of worship, the results are very bad indeed.

One sunny morning in the year 1969, when my wife and I were living at Alcott Bungalow in a quiet corner by the seaside in the Theosophical Estate at Adyar, near Madras, a glamorous young queen, named the Maharani of Jind, came unexpectedly to our door. We had met her the year before at the first Sai Baba World Conference in 1968 at Bombay -- where, to the many thousands present, Sai Baba announced his identity as an Avatar of the divine. As he made the announcement, the lights went off dramatically and came on by themselves a few minutes later. This signal of the lights, untouched by man, seemed to give a powerful significance to the announcement.

The Maharani of Jind was the step-daughter of Bulbir, our old and special friend from Horseley Hills, where we had had a magical time with Swami and a few of his followers in the summer of 1967. [1] We had come to know her very well and addressed one another by personal name. Hers was Prithvi. Consequently, her unexpected appearance one morning, in her

---

1 See my account of this in the book *Sai Baba, Man of Miracles.*

gleaming white sari, was a real delight to us. She soon revealed the purpose of her visit. She had come to show us the lingam Swami had given her at the last Sivarathri. "You mean he gave you one from inside himself?" I asked, hoping I did not sound too surprised. "Yes, Howard."

"Gorgeous" is the word that fitted her dark, glowing beauty. I knew she was a divorcee and felt that, like her step-mother, she was striving hard to live a spiritual dharmic life. I doubted if she was deeply steeped in the knowledge and practice of the Hindu religion. Deep down, I felt some uneasiness about her future welfare. "I understand that such lingams require a good deal of ritualistic attention, Prithvi," I remarked. "Yes," she replied, "Swami told me what to do and I shall do it." With that, she took from her handbag a roll of white silk and, unwrapping it, she laid it on the table, the lingam lying on the white bed of silk. It was a rich, reddish-brown color and perhaps a little smaller than an ordinary hen's egg. It glowed with a living radiance. Both Iris and I knew that we must not touch such an item. We stood looking at it admiringly and I had the distinct impression that it was looking at me. "It's so beautiful," Iris breathed. Prithvi smiled and, wrapping the white silk around her treasure, put it back in her handbag. "May it bring you great happiness and prosperity," I said.

Iris invited Prithvi to stay for lunch but she declined, saying that she had to get back home to Delhi but, as she had been passing through Madras, she could not resist giving us a quick visit in order to share her great joy with us. Gracefully, she walked away across the grass, turning to give a farewell wave before she disappeared into the greenery that led to the gate of the estate.

Remembering the event now, I recall the line of Keats: "A thing of beauty is a joy forever." The joy that remains in my heart is not the gleaming beauty of the red-brown lingam but the living beauty of Prithvi as she was on that sweet, smiling morning before the misfortunes came to her.

Every time we saw her at Prashanti Nilayam ashram after that, her beauty seemed to have faded more and more. Eventually we hardly recognized her. We heard from her step-mother some of the terrible, tragic things that happened in her personal life and the great misfortunes in her business affairs. It must have been worse than we heard, we decided, to have affected her appearance so drastically. Was it the influence of the gleaming red-brown lingam? I wondered. Perhaps, as I had suspected, she was not giving it the necessary pujas or ritualistic worship. Yet Swami had given her the lingam, so perhaps her great misfortunes were part of the karma she had to endure. But how long would it be before Swami would release her from it?

The day came when he did release her. The story of that release is a fantastic one. My wife and I were not at the ashram at the time, but I have read more than one account of it in print. Since accounts vary in detail, I was determined to get the facts from Prithvi herself as soon as the opportunity arose.

One day, seeing the Maharani of Jind among the visitors at Prashanti Nilayam, we thought: This is our chance. The strangely dramatic story was still clear in her mind and she told it readily. But, she said, in case she got one or two details wrong, we should ask her stepmother, who was also at the ashram. In fact, Bulbir was now there permanently, serving as the senior woman volunteer responsible for the discipline and good behavior of all the women visitors to the ashram. Though now grey-haired, she was still a stately, handsome woman, known to the other volunteers and most of the visitors to the ashram as *Mataji*, which means respected mother. We were very happy to do as Prithvi asked and call on our old friend to go over once more the story her stepdaughter had related.

We found her in the old guest house behind the Mandir, in the very room I had occupied when I first went to the ashram. So, with Bulbir's confirmation of the story, I felt I had the details correct, incredible though they were. Briefly, here is the story of how the Siva lingam was taken from the Maharani of Jind:

Swami called Bulbir and Prithvi, along with two or three other women, into the interview room which he often used in the old days, but does no longer. The room lay at the eastern, or bazaar end, of the veranda, with Swami's small dining room on the floor above it. Connecting the interview room with the dining room above was a sharply curved flight of stone stairs. Across the foot of the stairway, concealing it from the interview room, hung a thick green curtain. I have known strange things to happen behind that curtain, and even stranger in the dining room above. Through the solid floor once came tulsi leaves from the hand of Swami who was in the dining room above. They fell on the shoulders of Mr. Butt as he stood with Iris and me on the floor of the interview room awaiting Swami's return downstairs. [2] The leaves, that had actually taken the pain away from his heart, had come through the solid ceiling above us. Now something even stranger was to happen.

After talking to the group of women for a short time, Swami took Bulbir and Prithvi to the bottom step of the stairway and closed the thick curtain behind them. I know from experience that nothing spoken behind that curtain can be distinguished by people sitting in the interview room. Swami stood facing the two women, a couple of steps higher up the stairs. First he spoke briefly of the terrible things that had been happening to Prithvi since the lingam had been in her possession. Since they knew of his powers, the women were not surprised that he knew all about those things. He gave them to understand, beyond any doubt, that it was the lingam that had been bringing her this terrible misfortune. It had become very inauspicious, he said, because she had neglected to carry out, constantly and regularly, the ceremonial worship required to keep the lingam auspicious. He said this in a kindly, understanding way, blaming the circumstances of her life, with its increasing upheavals, on the neglect of the lingam that had taken things from bad to worse.

---

2 See my account of this in the book *Sai Baba, Man of Miracles.*

He told Prithvi that what he must do now was take the lingam away from her, but in its place he would give her a beautiful golden-colored shaligram. This was much bigger and more attractive than the little red-brown lingam. It would be safer for her because it did not require the same strict attention as the lingam.

But, at the thought of losing the lingam, Prithvi burst into tears. Whatever its effects had been, she could not bear to part with it. She wept with uncontrollable sorrow, like a mother who had grown to love a crippled child that caused her nothing but pain. Swami, with infinite compassion for her grief, did not ask her to open her handbag and hand the lingam to him. Using his supernormal power, he withdrew the lingam invisibly from the bag and substituted the gold shaligram. Then, for reasons known only to himself, he seems to have sent the lingam upstairs into the dining room. Judging from his kindly, sympathetic expression and silence, Prithvi concluded that Swami was letting her keep the lingam. She dried her eyes and smiled. Then suddenly she sensed that her handbag was heavier than usual. Opening it quickly, she saw that her red-brown treasure had vanished and in its place lay the big gold-colored shaligram. Then she burst into more uncontrollable weeping. The lingam had evidently gone back to the Unmanifest from whence it came and she would never see it again.

But suddenly there was a great crash in the dining room above. It could even be heard by the women waiting out in the interview room. To some it sounded as if a very great heavy stone had dropped on the floor of the dining room. To others it seemed like the crashing of a pile of crockery. Others heard a mixture of violent noises as if the room above had been shaken by an earthquake. This was followed by the sound of something coming down the stone stairway. Incredibly, it was the little red-brown lingam. It was not rolling but skipping from step to step. They saw it negotiate the sharp curve in the stairs, as if it were something alive, and then jump joyously from step to step towards them. But, though it seemed to have a will of its own, it did not go as far as the one whose desire had brought it back, but stopped and lay quietly at the feet of its master, Sai Baba.

Both women thought Swami wore a surprised expression but, leaning over, he picked up the lingam and holding it towards Pirthvi, he said "Your great desire for it has brought it back. So now take it, have both." A look of happiness lit the startled, tearful face of the Maharani of Jind as she wrapped her treasure again in its white silk covering and placed it back in her handbag. Then they all went beyond the curtain to join the women in the interview room. Swami opened the outer door to show that the interview was over and, saluting his feet, they all left the room.

As soon as they were in her stepmother's room, Prithvi opened her handbag to look again at her beautiful lingam. But the white silk wrapper was empty. The lingam had vanished. Prithvi's first impulse was to rush back to Swami, but she knew that would be of no use. The episode was over. By now he would probably have de-materialized the lingam and sent it back to the Unmanifest. In any case, they could not see him unless he invited them, and why should he do that? Her stepmother assured her that Swami had done the right thing and done it in the kindest way possible. "You should be very glad and thankful that he has lifted the burden from you," she told Prithvi. Deep in her heart, Prithvi knew this was true. By the time she was telling the story to my wife and me, big changes had already come into her life. The stormy times were over, both in her personal affairs and her business life. Her ship of destiny had moved into calm seas. Looking back, she told us it was hard for her to understand the overpowering attachment she had felt for the little shiny stone with its killing beauty.

I have related here the facts of the Prithvi story as both she and her stepmother gave them to us. But many things are difficult to understand. Why should this oval-shaped object, symbolizing the beginning of creation, have such power for good or evil in a person's life? And why should this power be auspicious or inauspicious depending on the behavior of its owner? Moreover, in the case of this particular lingam, what is the explanation of the conscious life it seemed to show when coming down the stairs? Sai Baba himself stated to the Maharani of Jind "Your desire for it has brought it back to you," and the manner of its return was not just an inanimate roll down the stairs, but an animate jumping from step to step. This seems more than just a sleeping consciousness in mineral life. Had a more advanced consciousness somehow been stirred within the energy patterns of the stone? Or does some form of spirit life attach itself to the lingam? And does this spirit need to be propitiated by ritualistic worship in order to keep it on friendly terms with the people, or person, associated with the lingam?

It is taught that some devic forms in the world of spirit require sacrificial or ritualistic worship to keep them on good terms with man. Perhaps the lingam has an attaching spirit of this nature.

6

HE HAS COME AGAIN

It is natural for a person to feel loyalty to a particular name and form of the divine, especially if, through custom, his mind has become conditioned that way. From childhood, I was taught to worship Jesus; I felt a twinge of disloyalty when I began to worship Sathya Sai Baba as God. Oddly, I also felt a little disloyal to Shirdi Sai who had grabbed my heart before I knew the Sathya Sai form. But Swami began to show me the deeper truth about this in two ways: First, by his parables in action -- which is what I call his miracles. There are many of these. In our early Sai days, we took a Christian woman to Swami for a healing of a difficult malady. He healed her and produced a small medallion for her with Christ on one side and himself on the other. Since then I have seen him do the same for other people as well as materialize other Christian symbols, such as figures and crosses. Without words, he thus teaches an important lesson. Second, he constantly teaches on the theme that there is only one God, though people call Him by many names. The one God answers to all.

Forms -- we begin to see -- belong to time. They pass with time but the true God behind them is eternal. How absurd it is to think that God might disapprove when we worship Him in one form instead of another. In order not to slip back into that strange idolatry, we must constantly keep our minds on the reality behind the forms. With that in mind, how should we think of Christmas?

We celebrate an event when eternity stepped into time. Many years ago, God took human form -- as he had done many times before in the long history of mankind. His purpose in coming was the same as it had always been -- "To raise the sons of earth," as the carol says.

During World War II, I had the good fortune to be stationed in Palestine for a few months and I visited Bethlehem. We drove from Jerusalem through countryside that looks somewhat like the country around Puttaparthi. We arrived at the little town of Bethlehem, which sits on a hill, the Church of the Nativity dominating the skyline. The church is built on the spot where once stood the inn that had no room for the birth of a Godman. Fortunately, the stable where the Christ-child was born still exists -- an underground stable beneath the inn. When I visited, the underground grotto was like an altar -- a mass of lights and burning candles. Perhaps it is the holiest altar in all Christendom. On the wall was an inscription in Greek (the Greek of the early Christian period) which identified for the visitor the spot where the manger stood, where the baby Jesus was laid on the straw. The atmosphere was sacred -- a holy vibration in the grotto where God once made his advent on Earth, humbly amongst the oxen.

It was a lowly beginning to an epoch-making event. There are some parallels with Sai Baba. Tradition has few stories about the boyhood and early manhood of Jesus, but we know a little about the time before his mission to mankind began, at about age thirty. His mission was of peace and love and righteousness. He showed the same compassion for sufferers that Bhagavan shows today and, like Swami, he had the miraculous power to help many of them. Jesus also demonstrated the power of divine consciousness over nature and over what we call "the laws of nature." He turned water to wine and walked on the waters of the lake. All readers of the New Testament know those stories. As a child, I believed them. Later, modern education led me to doubt them. Only when I saw the miracles of Swami did I again believe the Christian miracles.

One of many instances in which Swami changed his own image to that of Jesus, and vice versa, is shown in the experience of my friend Elvin Gates. During an interview in 1987, Sai Baba first revealed to Nalin Sedera, a young Sri Lankan man, that he was, in fact, Vivekananda reborn. Elvin was happy to be there for that event, and even happier when Swami manifested for him a splendid ring on which showed Sai Baba's own image. After giving the ring to Elvin, Swami took it back with the words, "No, you prefer the form of Jesus," which, of course, at that time was true. Holding the ring in his hand, Swami blew on it and the form of Jesus replaced that of Sai Baba.

Two things stirred the interest and excitement of the crowds outside the *mandir* that day. They heard that Nalin Sedera was Vivekananda and many followed him. Others saw Elvin's spectacular ring and followed him for a long time, asking to see the ring. He held it up for all to see, then hurried to his residential unit. I think now, after years, he has come to love the form of Sathya Sai Baba more than any other. He has become aware, of course, that the form of God is no more than a symbol of the great reality, although it is a very inspiring symbol. The two forms of Sai Baba, Shirdi and Sathya, and the form of Jesus as artists picture him, are but symbols of the same reality.

Many spiritual truths that Jesus taught then, Sai Baba teaches today,
expounding on them, giving a different emphasis to suit the modern age. Some are not easy for human nature to follow and few people have lived by them during the centuries between the two advents. "Turn the other cheek," for example. Do not return violence for violence. Give love where you find hatred. Love your enemies or those who despitefully use you. Do not dwell on the faults of others. Look instead to your own failings and correct them. We could go on finding parallels. Even one of Bhagavan's main themes, the divinity of man, was taught by Jesus: "I am in the Father, just as you are in Me and I am in you." "The kingdom of God is within you." A few other such statements have come down to us. Now Bhagavan Sai Baba emphasizes that truth -- a truth that modern churches have not taught.

Perhaps, as Tennyson said, "The thoughts of men have widened with the progress of the sons," and human consciousness has evolved to the level where it can accept the fact that we are all children of God with a divine inheritance awaiting us. All we have to do is brush aside the clouds of mortal sleep and remember our identity. But, is that so easy? I like the story from the Hindu scriptures about the prince who, as a baby, was kidnapped by robbers. He naturally grew up thinking of himself as one of the robbers. If someone had told him he was really a prince, would he have believed it? I think not. He would have needed proof. In the end, proof came and the prince returned to inherit his kingdom.

We are in a similar situation. The king himself has "come to the robbers' den," (an appropriate name for this world), to tell us we are his children. Won't we believe it now and act accordingly?

Love is the main theme of both incarnations. Love is the keynote on Christmas Day. Saint John, who was close to Jesus, wrote, "We love each other because He first loved us." Doesn't that truth echo in our hearts today -- now that God is here again and we are able to experience divine love? If sometimes we fall short of the ideal of loving each other, we know that the Sai family must strive to establish a nucleus of loving brotherhood as an example and inspiration to the world. What hope is there otherwise?

The lamp lit by the great teacher of Palestine shone through the Dark Ages in Europe, when the Kali Yuga was at its lowest ebb. It shone in the monasteries and cathedrals and in the lives of a few true Christians. Without that lamp, who knows to what levels of brutality and barbarity the world might have sunk? For the dark forces are always there within us, ready to drag us down to the brute level. But the lamp was there as a beacon to help mankind keep its upward course. Yet now, after two thousand years, the light grows dim. The churches stand empty and the forces of fear, suspicion, greed and hatred are gathering around a nuclear banner. The threat to man's existence on Earth and to the divine plan is greater than ever before. So God has come again to relight the lamp and guide us through the mortal storm. Or perhaps to quell the storm as he once did long ago on the Sea of Galilee.

The Child, the Lamp, the Victorious One of Christian imagery is the way we might see God. And going to the Hindu imagery in one of the *Puranas*, the gods say, "Siva himself is here playing the active role of his son, Subramanyam." The Father is the Son, the Son is the Father. All we know is that there is only one God, no matter what form or facet He reveals to us. On such deep matters, there is little we can know for sure. We can, however, feel some of the wonder of celebrating that long-ago advent in Palestine here at the birthplace of the Sai Avatar. The name "Jerusalem" means a place of peace, as does the name "Prashanti Nilayam." There is a place of peace within each one of us if we can find it.

In a song Denis Gursten wrote recently, one verse says:

So turn your weary eyes towards the Jerusalem within,
Where love is always burning now until the end.
Yes, turn against the darkest night and let His light shine in.
Turn around Jerusalem, He has come again.
Turn around Jerusalem, His glory's on the wind.
He has come, He has come, He has come again.

Yes, He has come and if you can receive it, know that the Eternal [1]One in the garb of Sathya Sai Baba is sitting here before you now.[2]

One Christmas day, I was honored by being asked to give a short preliminary speech before Swami spoke. Since it was Christmas, I gave the different names by which Jesus had been known: Joshua in his own country; Jesus by the Greeks; Yesu by the Celts, who had prophesied his coming in their scriptures called the "Triads;" Isu in Tibet; and Isa in India and the Middle

East, including Egypt.   (Incidentally, in the Battle of Alamein, the Australian Ninth Division was fighting over the Hill of Jesus as they called it, putting into English the Egyptian name Tel-el-Isa. I was pleased that it was the forces of my own country that drove the soldiers of tyranny from the Hill of Jesus.)

When I had finished the address, Swami stood up to give his discourse. He began by saying that Isa was the best name for Jesus because the three letters of the name, when rearranged, make the word "Sai." This brought great applause from the huge audience in the Poornachandra.

To conclude this chapter, let me say that when two authors of spiritual books, Peggy Mason and her husband Ron Laing, asked Swami during one of their first interviews if he were the Second Coming, his answer was in the affirmative. But, he pointed out then -- and at future times -- that being an Avatar of the highest God with form, known in India as Easwara or Mahaeaswara or sometimes simply Siva, he was what the Christians and Jews call "God the Father." Jesus, not being a full Avatar, was known as the "Son of God." But, Sai Baba pointed out firmly, whatever form is taken and whatever name is used, there is only one God. The Father is the Son and the Son is the Father.

7

WHY FEAR?

"Why fear when I am here?" This simple question often came from the lips of Sai Baba during his life at Shirdi and also during his present life. There is a wealth of meaning behind the simple question. Let us look first at the deeper meaning within the pronoun "I." As he knows himself to be an *Avatar* of God, he means when God himself is present, why should one fear? But that does not necessarily mean God in the form of Sathya Sai Baba. He teaches us and gradually we come to accept the amazing truth that God is within everything, within every atom of everything. So God is ever-present. Indeed, nothing else is ever-present. He is "here" wherever you happen to be. So the question is: "Why ever fear?" You should never fear, you should never be afraid because God is always with you and, being with you, he will take you safely through the very thing you are afraid of. In fact, nothing can happen to you that will not be for your own good in the long run. You should therefore live your life without a trace of fear, remembering that "I" is everywhere.

We can back up this happy conclusion by looking at another meaning of the pronoun "I." This comes, likewise, from Sai Baba's teaching of the Vedantic truth that God himself is within you, within everyone. Therefore, when you or anyone uses the pronoun "I," it refers to the God within. We may think of it as meaning your body or your individual ego, but it really means your true Self, or the God within. So certainly God is wherever you are. Being within your very soul as well as within every cell of your body, every atom of air you breathe, every blade of grass beneath your feet, He is indeed omnipresent. We could, therefore, rephrase the question thus: "Why are you ever afraid when the truth is that 'I,' God, am always present?"

But even if we know and accept these great spiritual truths, will we remember them and be calmed by them when a little fear is niggling at us or a great fear is making us tremble in every limb?

Let us next take a look at the anatomy of fear.

Under the label of fear can be placed that range of emotions from the powerful terror or panic that made the men of old times bolt for their lives when they heard -- or thought they heard -- the thundering hoofs of the great god, Pan. They range from devastating emotions that blind the mind, through a range of lesser fears, to the little worries or apprehensions that nag our minds consciously or sub-consciously throughout our waking hours. There is no doubt that this lesser brood of little fears or worries spoils the peace that should always be ours -- and cause many diseases.

I myself, like most people I know, have experienced the gamut of fear. I have never taken to my heels and bolted at the sound of the thunderous hoofs of the god Pan, but I have not been far from bolting in the face of the modern hoofs of Pan, as provided by modern warfare. From such experiences one learns valuable lessons.

One day, during the great battle of Alamein in the Eqyptian desert, I had taken a couple of war correspondents to see Major General Gatehouse, who was commanding the Tenth Armoured Division of the British Army in the Alamein line. One of the correspondents had been a friend of Gatehouse when they were both subalterns in the army during World War I. So we expected some worthwhile news to be revealed through such a personal contact. Standing beside the army tank that served as the General's tactical headquarters, he was quietly showing us maps and talking about his understanding of the current position of the battle, when suddenly an enemy artillery bombardment began. The General's tanks, scattered across the desert sands, were the target of the attack and it seemed to me that the General's headquarters' tank, beside which we stood, was the main target. Shells began bursting uncomfortably close to us. I expected this old veteran of two World Wars, along with a few young staff officers who stood round, to do as every soldier is trained to do: to go as flat as possible onto the earth. By such action, the smallest possible target is offered to the flying shrapnel. But the General continued to stand calmly upright in his cavalry boots, treating the attack with contempt, as if it were no more than a light shower of rain. This meant, of course, that his staff officers had to do the same. Whatever they may have felt, they had to stand there as if nothing untoward was happening. I don't know how my war correspondents felt, but I know that I was filled with fear. Furthermore, it seemed a madness to be exposing ourselves in this way when we could all have flattened ourselves on the earth in a nearby hollow. But I was afraid to appear cowardly by making the first move when the General and his staff seemed to be ignoring the bombardment.

The shells came closer. Any moment one of them whistling overhead would land near enough to wipe out the whole group of us. But the General continued to show us his maps and to talk calmly while his officers stood by in respectful silence. My fear grew very close to the panic that forces ones legs to bolt. But my will forced me to hold on and make no move that would lower my prestige before my brother officers and the war correspondents -- to say nothing of the steel-nerved divisional commander. I began to hope and pray that the bombardment would cease but, instead, it seemed to intensify. One tank on the exposed plateau of sand had been hit and was burning. This only made the General curse angrily that his tanks were exposed in a forward position, through the Army Commander's orders, instead of playing the role the tanks were meant to play.

His fearless anger about his precious tanks did not help the terror of death or mutilation that filled every cell of my body. Then my powerful, primitive terror seemed to reach saturation point and something entirely different took its place. The "something" is hard to put into words. I felt that I had risen to a vantage point above the scene of bursting shells, spouting sand and the burning tank. The scene lay in some remote dimension, while I sat in a place of bliss beyond time and space, watching the drama below as if it were no more than the replay of some ancient battle. I had, I suppose, reached what is known as "the moment of truth." I can say now, in retrospect, and with the benefit of the Sai inner views of life that came to me later, that I had moved out of my temporary ego into my true Higher Self, into the eternal Reality for which death in battle concerns only the body and not the real Self.

Lord Krishna pointed out this deep truth to his friend, the warrior Arjuna, at the battle of *Kurukshetra* long ago. If other men -- when saturated with the raw, primitive fear of facing death-dealing shot and shell -- have this transcendental experience, I understand why old soldiers love the memories of the actual battlefield. I only know that throughout the rest of World War II, at times when menacing bullets and shrapnel were slicing the air around me, I never felt any fear of death. Yet a strong fear lingered: the fear of damage to my eyesight. This was perhaps due to an intuition that my book of *Karma* held an entry of such damage in its future pages.

No doubt, I was fortunate. A saturation of primitive fear on that battlefield fifty years ago brought me to an awareness of the truth of being, which could be called a realization of the God within. He is closer to us than our own breathing because He is our very Selves. I ruminate now on the truth that if I could have been fully aware of my own divinity from the beginning, I would have had no fear. So, obviously, the object of spiritual learning is to become constantly aware of the fact that God is always in our presence. The question is why we should ever have fear. As we become more and more convinced that we are part and parcel of the one eternal, omnipresent God, we will know for sure that nothing can put a full stop to our existence or do us any real harm.

But, leaving aside the great fears -- the hammer blows of fate that may strike us at any time during peace, as well as war -- let us consider the little fears that are seldom, if ever, absent from our minds. Apprehensions, anxieties, all kinds of worry, whether in the foreground or the background of our waking hours, are unfortunately part of our daily lives. Swami has often said to me and others through the years, "Do not worry about anything. Just be happy." Gradually this simple, yet profound, formula for right-living sinks into the mind and one tries to practice it. Certainly, if one never worries about anything, one will always be happy, because that is the nature of man. But how do we prevent the worry or wipe it out when it comes? Surely the recipe is the same as that of dealing with great fear. That is, to cultivate a constant awareness of the presence of God within us and, indeed, of our identity with Him. That is much easier said than done. One cannot expect to reach such a state of wisdom overnight. It can only come gradually through the constant daily practice of the Yogic and spiritual exercises that Sai Baba and the other great ones have taught. Yet the result is certain: life completely free of all fear, a life of constant happiness.

I have spent many years either close to Sai Baba or thinking seriously and as deeply as possible about him. I have never seen him affected by the slightest trace of fear. Being fully aware of his Godhood, he knows that whatever he sets out to achieve (and it is always for the ultimate good of mankind), he will achieve. Being fully aware of his divinity, he knows that he cannot fail. The "slings and arrows" from the hands of the little men of darkness glance harmlessly from the amour of his divine confidence. His constant joy is shown in the ready laughter that waits just beneath the surface of his loving, compassionate eyes.

The pathway of our lives leads us in the direction of becoming as glorious a God-realized being as he is. That is our goal -- certain of ultimate achievement. Why be victims of fear when God is ever near? He is "nearer to us than breathing, closer than hands and feet." For He is our very Self.

8

FINDING AND GUARDING THE PRICELESS PEARL

The door opened a little, revealing a unique figure. "Are you the man from Australia?" he asked me with smiling eyes and a row of strong white teeth. But he did not wait for the answer -- which he probably knew already. Seeming to forget me, he moved into the room and went to two Indian gentlemen, the only other occupants. I looked at his long red robe and great mop of vibrant hair, but this did not tell me that he was the great Sai Baba I had come to see. At that time, in March, 1965, I had never seen a photo of Sai Baba even though I had been in India for six months. I think there were very few photographs of him circulating then. That morning, I had come to a house in Madras where I was told that Sai Baba was staying. As I watched him materializing vibhuti with a wave of his hand and patting one of the Indians who had dissolved into Bhakti tears, I realized this must be the miracle worker I had come to see. Now, as I write these lines thirty years later, I know, as I did not know then, that I had come to a great milestone in my journey. Not, indeed, to the end of my search for God, but to a point where the end would come clearly in view. I was fifty-eight years old. Why had it taken me so many years to reach this place in the great journey which had begun back in my youth? It had been an on-again, off-again search through the early phases. Like Parsifal's search for the Holy Grail, it had sometimes been forgotten and neglected for long periods of time. It had really only settled down in earnest continuity when I met Iris seven years earlier. I know now that we needed to be partners in this -- mankind's only important, essential journey. Also, as Swami says, there is a time for everything for each individual.

A good Sai friend of mine told me that my book, *Man of Miracles,* had been sitting on his bookshelf for ten years before he took it down and opened it. Then he began without further delay looking for a Sai Center that he could attend; that was a quick stepping stone to the *darshan* line at *Prashanti Nilayam* where he sat "to look into the eyes of God," as he puts it, at the age of sixty. That was his right time.

The case in which the time factor plays a very definite, though inexplicable, part is that of Colin Best, about whom I wrote in my book, *Where the Road Ends*. Briefly, Colin was told while in meditation that a world spiritual teacher even greater than Jesus was on earth, but that Colin would not come to this great teacher for another fifteen years. He did not have the patience for such a long wait so, being an experienced out-of-body traveler, he went in his astral body over India, considering this the most likely place to locate the great teacher. Guided by a light, he came to a building which he thought was a temple and, entering through a wall, he saw a fuzzy-headed man sitting on a stage before a big crowd of people. Though the man invited him into the hall, he was unable to move any further than the inside of the wall. Nor could he discover the identity of the fuzzy-headed one or the name of the place to which his guiding light had led him. So he returned to his body in Sydney. Exactly fifteen years later, as if by accident, he came across a photo of Sai Baba in a book and learned his name and whereabouts. Then, as soon as possible, he packed his bags and went to India to visit Sai Baba's *ashram*. His time had come to be a Sai Baba devotee.

Of course, it must be said that the time it takes us individually to come to the *Avatar* in this life is almost certainly the final lap of a journey that began many lifetimes ago. For whether or not man is consciously aware of the fact, the only journey of necessity throughout his many incarnations is that involved in the search for God. Only when this journey is accomplished is he finished with his sojourns on Earth. Of course, one's first darshan with Sai Baba, whether at the ashram or in a dream or a vision, is only the beginning of the last leg of one's odyssey to the Divine shores. On this vital phase of the journey there are sure to be many problems and obstacles -- even great tempests that will wreck the traveler's ship and leave him grimly clinging to a raft of faith in a stormy sea.

The first problem may be, as it was to me, the search for the light of understanding in a dark cloud of ignorance. "Many of us see Sai Baba as an Avatar," said the Prince of Venkatagiri as we sat together on a bench at Prashanti Nilayam during my first visit there in 1966. The bare-footed saint in the red robe walked across the brown sands some distance away. This unexpected remark felt to me like a blow below the belt. I really did not know exactly what an Avatar was. I did not answer the Prince, but decided then and there to study all the books I could find in the library of the Theosophical Society headquarters at Adjyar near Madras, where my wife and I lived at the time. But this research did not get me very far. The books mainly dealt with super beings such as Rama and Krishna, who lived long ago in the mists of time. They did not bridge the yawning gap between the eternal almighty God of the Universe and this small human figure with the sweet, smiling face, moving about in an ashram hidden away in the remote interior of India. Can the ocean be poured into a small bottle? Can the universe be squeezed into a grain of sand? I asked myself.

Of course, I was already aware that there was more than could be contained in the small, five-foot-two body in the flaming red robe, but this did not make him God, or at least my concept of God at that time. So for many months, I wrestled with the concept of Avatar.

Being with Swami a good part of the time in those years, I came to realize beyond any doubt that he was some kind of super being, but I was unable to conceive him as the great and only God of the universe. There is no doubt that he knew my problem, and it may have been partly for my benefit that he made a remark one morning to somebody else that enabled me to turn a corner. Of course, now I know that he helps many people at the same time with one word or phrase or sentence. I happened to be standing nearby when a very determined young Indian asked Swami point blank: "Are you God?" Swami could have simply answered,

"Yes," as he had done on many occasions. But, instead, pointing his finger at the young Indian, he said, "You are God." Then he began to elucidate the deep teaching that has been known to the few over the centuries, but not to the masses. In a nutshell, the teaching is that at our innermost core, each of us is divine, but this core is covered up like an onion with many layers of *mayamic* ignorance and, until those layers of the onion of illusion are peeled off and we reach the very center of our being, we have not the slightest notion of our true identity. We know not that we are descents of the Divine One. We are Avatars -- unaware of the fact. We are, as one writer put it, gods with amnesia. The only difference between him and us, Sai Baba says, is that he is an Avatar of God and knows it, whereas we are Avatars and don't know it. Of course, knowing this fact experientially makes all the difference between living the divine life of giving and forgiving, and the ordinary, selfish human life of getting and forgetting, as he says. The great gap between us and Baba does not have to remain. His purpose here on Earth is to help us bridge it.

This teaching helped me to overcome the gap in my understanding. The Avatar concept became acceptable and, because I was living close to Sai Baba at the time, because I was witnessing his lifestyle and feeling his divine vibrations, I came to accept that he was nothing less than an Avatar. This was an important step forward on my inner path. My own understanding of the great Avataric being deepened as my inner view of him increased through those blessed years, so that my faith in the truth of my conviction strengthened steadily. I became sure that I had found the truth of **his** being and of all being. I had found the pearl beyond price. How very blessed I was, for reasons that I know not.

Of course, I was not the only one who held the priceless pearl in his palm. The possession of it made brothers and sisters of us all. As the years passed, however, I with all my brothers and sisters in Sai, had to face some violent attacks on our inner knowledge, some powerful tests of faith. Swami used to tell us that when the tree of faith is just a tender sapling, we should fence it all around to protect it from enemies -- against goats and cattle that will tear the tree to pieces or tread it into the ground. But when the tree of faith has grown in size and strength, the fence can be removed. Even so, at times the tree will be attacked by powerful enemies such as hurricanes and cyclones.

The big tests do not come until our tree of faith has grown in strength, yet I know some individuals whose faith did not survive one or another of the cyclonic tests. Their trees have been flattened to the earth. The priceless pearls they held have been knocked away into the muck and mire of the storm.

I have tried hard to analyse and understand the reason why this has happened. One basic reason for their failure to hold steadfast to their faith is that -- seeing Sai Baba in the form of a man -- they come to think that he is no more than a man; they measure his actions by a small human yardstick and judge him accordingly. They forget that his divine vision and understanding embrace the past and future of mankind, as well as the present, just as it embraces that of each individual among his followers. Right-action within the time scale of the great divine vision and understanding, may seem like wrong action to our very limited human vision and understanding. Even the great Uddhava of the *Srimad Bhagavata*, meeting Lord Krishna some time after the *Kurukshetra* war, criticized the Avatar for the great destruction of that war. This may have been a right judgment in human terms, but it was certainly wrong judgment in terms of the Avatar's wider knowledge of the future good of mankind. Udivar had the wisdom to climb down from his little seat of human judgment and was rewarded with the wonderful teachings contained in the *Udivar Gita*, which can be read in English in the great *Srimad Bhagavata.*

Unfortunately not all those who today judge the Avatar from the level of the little human seat, have the necessary humility and veneration that enabled Uddhava to rise above the human level. They do not see that the fault lies within themselves for trying to fit the short human measuring tape around the being of the measureless Avatar. They make the mistake that Yasoda made in trying to tie up the child, Krishna, with rope. She found that no rope was long enough to go around his small, childish body. And so, when the pearl of faith is lost through such human errors, how many painful years, indeed centuries, might pass before it is found again? God, who is eternal and has eternal patience, does not see time in the way we struggling mortals do.

9

DO WE NEED A GURU?

If, from its Sanskrit roots, we understand the word "guru" to mean one who dispels the ignorance from our minds, then it is simply synonymous with the word "teacher." We all need teachers and, of course, many such teachers or gurus touch our lives. But if we take the word to mean one who dispels the fundamental ignorance of our own identity, shows us the truth of our being and leads us all the way to God, then a guru is a very special person indeed. Such a person is often called a *sadguru* or a *paramaguru*. The question we will consider here is whether we need one such as this.

A story told by Sai Baba of Shirdi throws light on man's need in this regard. By "man," I mean one who has reached the point in his evolution when he feels the need to get his feet onto a spiritual path. Shirdi Sai brings himself into the story, but sometimes he did this in tales that were told simply as parables. Those might be true stories about himself -- either in his present, or some earlier, incarnation. The story begins as Sai Baba of Shirdi and other young men walked in a forest. The young men discussed various aspects of spiritual philosophy and also debated the question of whether a spiritual aspirant needs a guru. As they walked and talked and argued in the dense forest, they became completely lost. Then they met a man who seemed to be a worker, perhaps a woodsman. He kindly invited the young men to his bush hut to eat; afterward, he said, he would guide them out of the forest. But unfortunately, the students were caste-conscious. They considered the woodsman a low-class, ignorant fellow, whereas they themselves had the benefit of higher learning. They refused his offer and walked on. Wandering in a circle, as those lost in a forest often do, they met the woodsman again. Magnanimously, he extended his invitation again, but in their pride of intellect and learning, the men again refused. But after they had gone some distance further into the forest, the young Sai changed his mind. He quickly retraced his steps and caught up with the woodsman. He apologized for the brusque refusal and declared humbly that he would like to accept the woodsman's offer of hospitality. Smiling with pleasure, the woodsman took the young Sai to his hut. Nearby was a well of water. The young Sai, who now felt impelled to submit to anything the woodsman prescribed for him, allowed his feet to be tied to a rope and then agreed to be suspended upside down in the well, his head almost touching the water. Then the woodsman went away, promising to return later.

In an hour or two, the woodsman returned and pulled the young Sai out of the well. Taking the young man inside his hut and seating him there, the woodsman asked how he felt. Sai replied that the experience in the well had brought him great bliss; in fact, he still felt it. The woodsman patted him affectionately, speaking to him in a voice which -- as Sai put it -- dripped with honey. Then he gave Sai pure, natural food to eat.

Sai had no wish to leave either the forest hermitage or the man. The man looked like a woodsman, but Sai knew instinctively that this was his *sadguru*. The young student's love for his spiritual preceptor continued to grow in strength as he sat at the master's feet, learning from him and serving him in every way he could. The intellectual discussions and debates that he had once enjoyed with his fellow students now seemed hollow and valueless.

The story just related has a number of symbolic meanings for those who would tread the spiritual path. The forest is the material world in which we live and which, to a large extent, is illusory. In Sanskrit, it is called *samsara*. The subject matter promotes many discussions and debates among people who, like ourselves, are anxious to shed light on the great mysteries of life and death, and the reality that lies beyond life and death -- in other words, the question: Why are we here? We go around in circles, just as the students in the parable did, becoming lost in the maze of our own minds. Such discussions can have no real value until they lead us to the sadguru who, because he knows the way out of the samsara, can lead us. But first it is necessary for us to turn our old worldly values upside down -- symbolized by the reverse position in the well -- and gain the necessary true knowledge which the great guru, in his divine love, will impart to us.

The student hangs by his feet with his head close to the water of wisdom which, though very close to him, the student is not yet able to drink. This symbolizes the austerities and denials we must go through in order to completely reverse our scale of values. In the words of Jesus, we must learn to store up our treasures in the spiritual world rather than on Earth -- where we must soon lose them and discover they have no value at all. They may have a little temporary value in the brief period we spend on Earth, but no value in eternity, to which we really belong.

The fact that only one of the young men came to the guru they met in the forest, teaches that no-one will come to his guru until he is ready; but then, he will certainly find his guru and recognize him. Sometimes the recognition is immediate, sometimes it takes a little while, as it did in the case of the young Sai.

You will naturally ask whether it is necessary for every individual to have a guru. Sathya Sai Baba answered, when we put the question to him, that in *some* life, it is necessary. I understand that to mean that in some lives, we are not ready for the paramaguru to take responsibility for our souls and stay with us to the journey's end. In other lifetimes, it may not be necessary because in the previous life we had such a guru and through his guidance we found our inner guru, or the God within ourselves. But if that God -- that inner God -- has not been fully realized, we will come to Earth again. Without an external guru, we will be able to reach full God-realization through our inner spiritual guide.

This was the case, I think, for the famous Ramana Maharshi of Aranuchula. When one of his followers asked him if he had had a guru, he replied that in a former life he had. Some other very advanced beings such as Aurobindo -- although they do not need a sadguru to take them to their goal -- seem to need some help from an outside being (who could be called a guru) to assist them in throwing off the clouds of *maya* that seem to hang around practically every being who comes into human birth.

Sai Baba of Shirdi seems to have needed two gurus in his youth, one a Muslim fakir and another a Hindu master, to scrape away the scales of *maya* that hid him from his realization of his own Godhood. In his next birth, however -- as Sathya Sai Baba -- he does not seem to need any kind of guru at all. Likewise, Krishna, the full Avatar of some five thousand years ago, did not seem to require a guru to awaken him to his own divine reality.

But apart from these great leaders of mankind, what about the ordinary sons of Earth? There is no doubt that all of us require a guru in the ancient Indian sense of a teacher, even if it is only our parents. I myself, for example, was taught farming by my father and the reality of the spiritual world by my mother. Later, I was taught other occupational skills by my teachers and more about the spiritual dimension by ministers of religion; but none of these would expect to be called gurus. But they are so in the sense that they remove the darkness of ignorance and bring knowledge and light to the mind.

But what about the higher guru who will take responsibility for our souls and lead us to journey's end? There comes a point in our long human pilgrimage of many lifetimes on Earth, when we hear a distant bugle call from our true spiritual home. It is a call we cannot deny, so we begin to struggle to find a pathway to that home. Books will somehow come into our hands and we will read them avidly, satisfying our hunger for the knowledge that will help our footsteps along the path. We may make progress and find out a great deal in this way. But we will encounter many obstacles that seem impossible to break through or circumnavigate. The books and spiritual helpers who come to us as if by accident, may not provide the answers we need because, within the perimeters of the great yoga pathways to God, each individual treads his own path. The only one who can help at this juncture is the sadguru -- the one who knows and can give the necessary help for each one's individual path. He is waiting somewhere ready to give his help.

How will you find him when you need him? There is a great spiritual law that says when the pupil is ready, the guru will appear. The young men wandering lost in the forest of *samsara* illustrate this. Only one was ready and he, after some hesitation, recognized his sadguru. When you find and come to him, you will be on what is called the *gurumarga* or the guru path. This comes within the pathway known as the *bhaktimarga* or the path of devotion. The unbreakable link between the guru and the pupil is that of divine love. Other things that are needed on this pathway, such as discipline and knowledge, will be supplied by the guru. But, in the end, it is the power of love -- and only this power -- that will bring you to the spiritual goal of reunion with the divine.

Does every aspirant for liberation and enlightenment need such a sadguru? As Sai Baba told us, in some life he does. If, in some former life -- probably the last one -- such a sadguru has led you through a deep enough recognition and acceptance of your own inner guru, then in this lifetime, you may be able to take the last few steps to self-realization without any outside help.

So the answer to the question, "Do we need a guru?" is this: All of us need many gurus in the form of teachers; some need a sadguru or a paramaguru. If this be the vitally triumphant lifetime when they are destined to make the breakthrough to the spiritual home, then bear in mind that only a very few rare individuals can do it alone.

10

THE REBIRTH OF VIVEKANANDA

One day in the late 1960's, probably 1969, when my wife Iris and I were sitting alone in a room with Sai Baba at one of his *ashrams*, he said in what seemed a casual manner, "Vivekananda has been reborn in Sri Lanka. When his education and training are complete, he will help me with my mission." Remembering the scene from over twenty-five years' distance, I don't think I really appreciated how blessed we were that Bhagavan should impart this great news to us. Not that I knew a great deal about Vivekananda at that time, but I did know that he was the acknowledged leader of a number of monks who took Paramahansa Ramakkrishna's pure spiritual message to the western world. Now Swami was telling us that Vivekenanda had come to earth again from the highest spiritual realms to take part in the Sai mission to mankind. What a mighty mission it must be with three incarnations of the Sai *Avatar* and the great sage Vivekananda to help! Was this news exclusive to us? I wondered at the time. But, no. A young American friend of ours, Andrew Schartz, told us later that Swami had made the same announcement to him and a few of his friends. Naturally word of such an event soon spread among Sai Baba's followers and Iris and I thought it was time we found out more concerning this world teacher, who had left his body in 1902 at the early age of thirty-nine, and who was now destined to play a part in the Sai movement.

Some years later, in our search for material, we came across a large volume called *The Gospel According to Ramakrishna.* This is an on-the-spot, almost day-to-day account of the great master's teachings to the group of young disciples who came daily to sit at his feet at Dakshineswar on the banks of the Ganges, not far from Calcutta. In my opinion, this book is a spiritual classic, written in a kind of diary form by one of the disciples who modestly calls himself "M." In its pages, we found a truly fascinating account of how the being later known as Vivekananda incarnated in the 60's of last century to head the team of monks who would carry the teachings of Paramahansa Ramakrishna beyond India to the four corners of the earth.

Considering the Master's frail physical body and the strenuous nature of travelling last century, he was not able to do the work of spreading his gospel himself. Vivekananda, with the help of other dedicated monks, did this for him after his death in 1886.

The vision that Ramakrishna related to his young followers came to him when he was in samadhi and is a vision of a past event -- the important event of how his mission to mankind began and how Vivekananda was drawn into it. This memory vision of the past, we are told, took him above the many celestial realms, some of them even inhabited by gods and goddesses -- in fact, above the whole manifest universe into an eternal realm that knows no dissolution. There he saw seven holy men sitting in a group absorbed in deep contemplation of Brahman. Next it seemed to him that a portion of the Absolute became a divine child. The child went and sat on the knee of one of the holy men. At the child's tender touch, the holy man opened his eyes and looked at the child with great affection. The child said that he would soon assume a human body and asked if the holy man would come down to assist him in his mission for the redemption of mankind. The holy man agreed to this. Sri Ramakrishna said that the holy man was Narendra and also declared, in answer to an inquiry, that he himself was the divine child.

Although in the physical body of his incarnation, the child Ramakrishna grew to manhood, he remained a child at heart to the end of his life. He was aware when the holy sage from on high incarnated on earth in a suburb of Calcutta, but the sage himself came to birth in such a thick veil of *maya* that like other human beings, he was completely unaware of his own identity. He was named Narendra and as he grew to manhood he showed himself to be a young man of remarkable character traits: He possessed great physical courage and presence of mind, a vivid imagination, a deep power of thought, keen intelligence and an extraordinary memory; he had a love of truth and a passion for purity, a spirit of independence and a tender heart; he was an expert musician and during his education acquired a proficiency in physics, astronomy, mathematics, philosophy, history and literature; even as a child he practiced meditation and showed a great power of concentration.

In due course he came to Ramakrishna's feet, guided, of course, by the inner knowledge of his purpose in life that lay deep within him. Ramakrishna, knowing that in reality his beloved Naren, as he called him, was a great sage, was afraid that if the young man broke through the maya and came to know his true identity, he may, in an act of true yoga, leave his body and return to his spiritual home. The master set out to train Narendra in the non-dualistic Vedantic philosophy, but Narendra, because of his religious training during his boyhood and early youth, considered it wholly blasphemous to look on man as one with his Creator. One day in the temple garden, he laughingly said to a friend, "How silly! This jug is God! This cup is God! Whatever we see is God and we, too, are God! Nothing could be more absurd." That was what he thought of his master's teaching on *advaita*.

Then Sri Ramakrishna came out of his room nearby and gently touched him. The effect was that he immediately perceived that everything was indeed God. A new universe opened around him. Returning home in a dazed state, he found that the food, the plates, the eater himself, the people around him were all God. When he walked in the street he saw that the cabs, the horses, the streams of people, the buildings were all Brahman, or the Absolute God. He could hardly go about his daily affairs. His parents became anxious, thinking he was ill. When the intensity of this experience abated a little, he saw that all around him was a dream. It took him some days to return to a state of the dualism necessary for normal operations in life. But he had had a foretaste of a great experience yet to come, and realized that the words of non-dualistic Vedanta were the truth. The experience was very rich and significant. He also realized that in the relative world, the need of a personal God is imperative.

Sri Ramakrishna was overjoyed with the conversion of his favorite pupil. It is hardly surprising that the student, in view of what he had been before his birth, became the leading pupil. After the death of the master, when all the unmarried students -- the vast majority -- decided to carry the master's teachings into wider fields, they all adopted spiritual names. Narendra became Vivekananda, the leader of the great mission.

Having gained this concept of his spiritual and intellectual greatness, learned of his inspiring powers of leadership, and read a good deal of Vivekananda's teachings, I was very eager to discover what his reincarnation would be like. Of course, he may not have the handsome body and brilliant mental powers of his earlier incarnation, but he would be equipped with whatever faculties and powers were necessary for his work in the Sai mission. I, like many others, awaited his appearance at Sai Baba's ashram. But the years passed and we heard no more.

When in the year 1987, the young man from Sri Lanka made his debut at Prashanti Nilayam in India, I was away in Australia. In March of that year, he came, along with a group of people from his own country. Wrapped in the veils of maya, he was completely unaware of his true identity -- as Narendra had been over a hundred years before. What a great shock was in store for him!

As it happened, a good friend of ours, an Australian, Elvin Gates, was in the interview room with a group that included some people from Sri Lanka -- Vivekananda incognito among them. Elvin Gates told us all he witnessed, which, unfortunately, was not much, because the great revelation had been made in the private interview room when the young man and his male friend were alone with Swami. After the interview, news quickly spread throughout the ashram and crowds began to follow the young man wherever he went; people even waited outside his door in one of the round-houses. This became such an inconvenience that

Swami directed the young man to move from the round-house to the students' hostel outside the walls of the ashram.

Two years later, in 1989, I was fortunate enough to hear something of the young Sri Lankan himself and get a partial report on what happened in the inner room during the two interviews that took place on two successive days in March, 1987. This came about because during our time with Swami in 1989, we went with him to his Brindavan ashram and were graciously given accommodations in his hostel inside the enclosure near his *mandir*. Our fellow guests for several weeks were Ravi Jai Warden and his wife Penny. We four became very good friends. We discovered that they knew the young man who had now been identified as Vivekananda reborn. While they lived in Colombo, Sri Lanka, the young man, whose name was Nalin Sedera, lived with his parents, two brothers and a sister just outside Colombo. While Nalin was not a close acquaintance of theirs, they knew that he was not an ordinary worldly young man but was, like themselves, on the spiritual path. He seemed to study a great deal and spent much of his time in meditation. In this way, at least, Nalin was like his previous incarnation, Narendra.

Later when Ravi learned that I was writing this chapter on the wondrous Vivekananda phenomenon, he was kind enough to approach the young man, Nalin, and seek information, letting him know that I was planning to use any information he gave. Nalin Sedera agreed, after considering and perhaps meditating on the matter, and while he certainly did not describe all that had taken place at the two interviews when the great revelation of his identity was made to him, what he did tell was of considerable interest and is revealing to those who seek the inner view of words and events.

He said that before coming to Sai Baba the first time -- still quite unaware of who he was -- he had had a dream in which Swami, dressed in a white robe, had shown him an old couple, telling him that these had been Nalin's parents in a former incarnation. The dream intrigued Nalin and he longed to know more about the parents and his former incarnation. Perhaps the dream was a precognition and preparation for the staggering revelation that he was soon to encounter in the interview room. When, however, the youth asked Swami to tell him more about his former parents, Swami's reply was, "Forget about that. I am your father and your mother." -- meaning, of course, his spiritual father and mother. The former parents were simply instruments of a former birth and it was not important for Nalin to know any more about them. Then Swami asked the youth, "What is your name?" It is strange that Swami often asks people to state their name, though he knows the answer full well. The youth replied, "Nalin." Swami said, "You are not Nalin; you are Naren." This was the name that Ramakrishna always used for his beloved disciple, Narendra. Then Swami said, "In your previous birth you were a great saint. Do you know who Narendra was?" Nalin replied, "No, Swami, I don't." Sai Baba went on, "Narendra was the name of Vivekananda."

From the sketchy notes that Nalin had made from memory of the interview, it seemed that Swami eased him gradually and gently into the knowledge of his identity. Nalin does not say what his inner reaction was, but he does say that he cried a great deal during this first interview, as, of course, he had every right to do.

At one stage, Swami asked the question he asks everybody. He said, "What do you want?" Nalin's reply was, "First I want you, Swami; I want your love and also I want a job." "Why do you want a job?" the Lord asked him. "For money," he answered. "Why do you want money?" Swami asked him, and there seems to have been no answer.

Two things said at one or the other of the two interviews give much food for thought. One is that Swami asked him when he was coming to live at the ashram. Nalin replied, "In the year 2021." That is the year in which Swami has announced he will leave his Sathya Sai body, to be reborn one year later as Prema

Sai. But, of course, it would be some years before the newborn Prema Sai would be old enough to lead the Sai mission. Does this mean, one wonders, that Nalin -- speaking with the knowledge and wisdom of the great sage who was his true Higher Self -- knew that his work would begin when Sathya Sai passed away -- as it did, incidentally, when Ramakrishna left his body? Did he know that his work on earth for mankind was to fill the gap between Sathya Sai and Prema Sai? That is, to fill the gap until Prema Sai becomes active as a spiritual leader. One could estimate that this could be about twenty years, between 2021 and 2041. This seems a reasonable speculation.

The other interesting, and somewhat surprising remark, is that Swami said to the youth, "I have been waiting for you for eighty-five years." As Vivekananda left his previous body in 1902, the interview that Sai Baba gave to Nalin was eighty-five years later in 1987, but in 1902 Sai Baba was active in his Shirdi body, so it must mean that Sai Baba had expected the return of the great sage from the end of his former life as Narendra/Vivekananda. But God does not command a sage or a saint any more than he commands us, his younger children. "In patience, he stands waiting," as the poem says. I have heard, incidentally, from one who knows his face well, that Nalin Sedera has been back to the ashram secretly and incognito more than once. In view of what happened to him on his first visit, when he was so pestered by the curiosity of the crowds, he needs a secrecy of movement in order to enjoy the presence and imbibe the love and grace of the great Avatar. This along with the privacy of study and meditation will, no doubt, be part of his necessary training for the great divine work that awaits him in future time.

11

LIFE AS ONE IN TRUTH AND PRACTICE

The greatest spiritual teachers of all ages, from Lord Krishna to Sathya Sai Baba today, have taught a truth that is not easy to accept at first. It is this: In spite of all appearances to the contrary, life is one. There is only one God or one absolute existence; everything that exists around us is part of that one existence, that one God. Usually in the past, this truth was taught only to the selected few who were ready to receive it. For example, in the Mystery Schools, or religions of the ancient world, those who were considered ready for such a truth were initiated into it by the hierophants. The masses were left to believe that what they saw with their eyes and heard with their ears -- the many forms of life and the many gods who rule from above -- were the truth of being. Today great teachers are casting such pearls of wisdom to the masses. They know, of course, that among the masses there are still many "wild dogs" who, in the words of Jesus, will turn to rend them. This is a risk they must take if they are to save the world and mankind from threatening disaster. Those whose feet are on the spiritual path accept this inner truth, not only because they have heard it from the great ones, but also because it rings true to the touchstone of truth within them -- the *Buddhi*, or intuitive mind.

But, though they may accept the oneness of all in principle, can they put it into practice in their daily lives? Can they arrive at and live by that shining ideal which seems so far above what is practicable in daily living? It is somewhat like the enticing bunch of grapes at the top of a high garden wall which the fox tried in vain to reach in Aesop's fable. When the highest jump he could make did not enable the fox to grasp the bunch of grapes, he appeased himself by saying that the grapes were probably sour anyway. He turned aside and went on his way.

Those of us who are struggling to put the high ideal of oneness, or unity, into practice in our lives are a bit like the fox. We fail again and again but we must not turn away like the fox and forget it, thinking that, as we cannot practice it, it cannot be the truth.

Yet it is fair to ask ourselves if the great ones who taught this truth practiced it in their lives themselves? Let us take a look at that important question. Paramahansa Ramakrishna, for example -- who taught a group of young disciples last century and whose teachings are still spread through the world by his followers -- taught that the great truth of existence was *advaita*, or non-duality -- that in truth, all life is one. But did this great master of the spirit live the advaita that he taught? Yes, in most respects he did, because his life was completely devoted to the uplifting of mankind. But, in one respect at least, he practiced dualism, or the duality which is opposite the non-duality he taught. After telling his pupils that the truth was non-duality, he would go and pray fervently to the divine Mother in the form of the goddess Kali. He understood fully what he was doing, he said, but excused himself by saying that, like an ant, he preferred the pleasure of eating sugar to becoming one with the sugar.

Another great teacher, Ramana Maharshi, lived and taught during the first half of this century in his ashram at the foot of the sacred mountain called Arunachala. Having reached the high state of self-realization in which it is known and experienced that all is one, he was an advaitist to the core. He taught a type of meditation which required no acceptance of dualism. But he did say that any of his followers who could not reach the goal in this way should employ the devotional path, that is, the *bhakti marga*. This calls for love and devotion to a great Being -- call him what you may -- and is without doubt a dualistic practice. In this way, Ramana Maharshi was similar to the great *rishi* of the eighth century A.D., Adishankara, who taught the Vedantic philosophy of advaita or non-duality. While expounding advaita as the deepest truth that man can reach, Adishankara did say that among the instruments and conditions necessary for liberation, "*Bhakti* alone is supreme." In other words, he seemed to say that, while advaita is the great truth of being, it may be like the bunch of grapes at the top of the wall. If you cannot grasp it, then you should use the dualistic bhakti path, where love of God is the ladder that helps you climb the wall. In other words, we must practice the dualism of divine worship and love in order to reach the truth of non-dualism.

Brought up in Christianity as taught in the churches, I was a dyed-in-the-wool dualist. I read such lines as those by Omar Khyam:

When all is one, where is the need for sorrow?
Or of that gaudy myth of thee and me,
These that we call yesteryear, today, tomorrow
Merge in the moment of eternity.

I loved the music of the poetry but wondered if it was more than the poet's dream?

When Sathya Sai Baba first cast this pearl of wisdom at my feet, I was more ready to receive it and meditate on its value.

Sai Baba says that his life is his message. Fortunately, I had his life before me to study and contemplate. In all the words and actions of his life, I never detected a selfish or self-centered motivation. The more I contemplated his daily life, the more certain I became that, while parts of it were hard to understand because his vision of life was so much greater than mine, I knew that all his actions were aimed in one direction -- towards the spiritual uplifting of mankind. Never did I see the slightest deviation from his path in his great mission. It seemed to me that he lived constantly within the wonderful truth of oneness (the unity of all life). His life and work aims to establish that great truth in the minds, hearts and lives of all who follow him. It is clear, however, that he does not expect us to be able to grasp that high bunch of grapes immediately. In his teachings, along the bhakti marga, or the bhakti Vedanta pathway, he employs the ladders of dualism to help us up the unscalable walls. For example, he teaches us to pray to a being beyond ourselves, that is, to God -- in whatever form and by whatever name appeals to our hearts. In fact, the more we pray, he says, the better we progress. Although he employs all the climbing irons of all the *yogas,* he teaches that an ever-increasing love of God is the great ladder that will take us to the top of the wall. So here we have the practice of duality in order to reach the ideal of non-duality.

The truth of this great ideal began to seep in more and more as my years passed on the Sai pathway. I began to see it reflected in other religious teachings, if only as a muted background. In Christianity, as in other Semitic religions, we are taught that God made heaven and earth. So all that are in them, including the separate souls, come from God and are a projection of Him, are part of Him. It seems that, according to this theology, they remain separate from Him for eternity, as indeed they do also in the teachings of the great Vedantins, Ramanuja and Mahadevin. They are of His essence and not really separate, although they appear to be.

It seems that the truth of oneness lies at the base of all great religions. Did not Jesus die on the cross to bring mankind back to at-onement with God? How did we come to forget this oneness of all and have to learn it over again? Different spiritual philosophies have different explanations for this.

At one end, there is the fascinating Garden of Eden myth, which shows man and woman made by God and given his own breath as their animating spirit. It shows them walking and talking with Him as their own father in the paradise of the Garden. By going their own way against the divine will, they lost their awareness of their oneness with God. All their descendants -- that is, mankind -- were born into the state of ignorance of their unity with the divine. I believe that is what is meant by original sin -- a state of forgetfulness into which we are born. We come into this state of obscuration, the veil of Isis of the Egyptians, the *maya* of the Hindus. It is a fog of the mind out of which we must find our way.

At the other end of the list of explanations is that of the great

Pythagorus who sees monads of consciousness coming like sparks from a fire from the great one Being, the one Existence beside which there is no second existence. The individual monads are parts of the One. They are sown as the farmer sows seeds in the soil of God's universe. If those monads had originally any memory of their oneness with God, they doubtless lose it when they begin their evolution and growth through the kingdoms of minerals and thence into the vegetable kingdom, climbing finally into the animal world and from there taking their step upward into the developed self-consciousness of man. Yet, even in that state, their link of memory with their divine origin has not yet been re-established. We human beings have to learn it the hard way in the school room of earth before we can take the next step upward.

Whatever the true explanation of how our link of memory was broken, the fact remains that we human beings are walking the earth completely unaware of our true divine identity. We think we are living in a world of strangers, some we like, some we dislike, some we love, some we learn to hate. The truth of the matter is that, like God himself, they are nearer than our own hands and feet. Every one of those strangers, from China to Peru, is one with our very Selves. Each is part of the divine breath that God breathed into man. Each is a seed of consciousness from the absolute consciousness of God. Each is a spark from the one divine fire. But even when we accept the truth of this in theory, as in the end all must, we have not reached the top of the wall where the blissful prize, the divine nectarine bunch of grapes is waiting. When we have reached it and tasted of the fruit, we will experience in our very being the blissful truth of oneness.

But how do we reach this shining goal of human life? Many people, especially those on the spiritual path, have unitary visions of oneness. My friend, Susan Austin, who is a very keen follower of Sai Baba, told me that once she was lying alone in a grassy meadow in a pensive mood. Suddenly she had a change of consciousness in which she saw everything as one. She was part of the oneness. "I was one with the grass, with the trees and the sky," she said. It was a wonderful experience but only lasted a minute or so.

I have written about my own unitary experience in another place. I will say here only that I was completely surrounded by the Light Divine, the *Jyoti*. All was one in the joy-giving light. After a while, I could see a landscape from the world in the distance. It seemed waiting to surround me again. I knew that the Light was a facet of the one God and was the Truth, and that the world of duality that soon encompassed me again was our necessary school room, but only a temporal reality.

Sometimes a unitary vision will completely change someone's life, as in St. Paul's experience on the road to Damascus. There he saw the Light and heard a voice from on high. He suffered blindness for a time and was healed in Damascus by one of the followers of Christ whom he had been persecuting. This brought a complete turn around in his life.

Perhaps the best illustration of the great ideal of oneness, or non-duality and the practical need for duality in this training ground of earth, is the story of Narendra (Vivekananda) given in the last chapter. Of course, although we are here enmeshed in duality, the knowledge of the truth of non-duality will flavor our lives and change our way of living. It must inevitably lead to peace, non-violence and universal love that are the expressions of oneness with all life.

There are a few on earth who, like Ramana Maharshi, can grasp the grapes of enlightenment in one jump, but the majority of us are like Aesop's disappointed fox who failed to make the grade. But we must not be like him and say the prize is not worth having. Even the highest and most sheer of walls can be scaled with the right equipment, technique, practice and determination. What equipment do we need to conquer this most formidable and most important wall in our life's journey?

First, we must have absolute belief in our goal. We must have complete faith that on the heights above us lies the great truth we are seeking. Equally important, we must have the courage and willpower to carry us upward through all dangers to the heights. These are an important part of the reliable equipment to sustain us. Although admittedly we cannot live the non-dualistic way in our day-to-day existence, we can strive to practice it more and more. All the techniques of spiritual discipline, known as *sadhana,* will help us in this. Some of these are prayer, meditation, study of the great scriptures, thinking, speaking, acting in selfless, loving ways, practicing sending love with open hearts not only to God in any form we can picture him, but to all human beings. All are embodiments of God.

One very powerful method for developing that love, which is the essence of oneness, is to give selfless service to our fellow men. Sai Baba encourages his followers to give more and more such service. There is need for it everywhere, but especially in war-torn, devastated countries. To paraphrase the statement of Jesus when he spoke of service: For as much as you have done it -- that is, for as much as you have given this help -- to the least of these my children, you have given it to me. We understand this better when we know that God is in all. In such service, happiness lies and the love of God increases. Such daily practices of sadhana provide the climbing irons for scaling the sheer wall.

At some point in the dizzy heights, when courage and confidence seem to be about to waver and faith has been tested almost to its limits, we will come to a ladder that has been let down from the top of the wall. This is the ladder of divine love and grace. It has come in response to the constant love and devotion to God we have shown in all our endeavors. With this he draws us to the top of the wall where we eat the divine fruit of enlightenment. Looking beyond the wall, we see a new world, for we have come into a new state of consciousness where all is one and separateness is a gaudy myth of the past. We may remain merged in this bliss of oneness, which is called nirvana, or we may, after a period, be called back across the wall by love of our fellow men to help them in their pain-racked striving to reach the same goal we have reached. Then we would be free souls in the world, without karma, and would be able to live in full consciousness of our oneness with all. We would see the apparent separateness in this world as a veil of illusion.

It seems to me that, although the truth of being is the oneness of all, its practice in this world, in this human life, can at best be only partial until we have reached our goal of enlightenment -- the realization of oneness. Then this truth can be lived in full either here on earth or in some spiritual realm. To remember fully who we are and live the life of divine love or oneness is the purpose of the soul's long pilgrimage on earth.

12

AT THE BROKEN HEART OF A CITY

We had been to Mexico City once and had no wish to return. The city, built on islands in a lake, no doubt was breathtakingly beautiful when the conquering Spaniards first beheld it, but the water was later drained and part of Mexico City rested on the lake bed. This caused some buildings to list at an angle even more critical than the Leaning Tower of Pisa. But that was not what we minded. We found the place too big (I have heard it is the world's largest), too noisy and its people glum and somber, neither friendly nor welcoming. Furthermore, since its altitude is over eight thousand feet (higher than any Australian mountain), we expected the air to be bracing and fresh. Instead, we found it more polluted than Los Angeles. The heavy motor traffic could account for this.

We remembered from the first trip how vehicles raced madly -- seemingly murderously -- along the great central avenue, Pasea de la Reforma, which has six main lanes with an extra on each side, bordered by lawns, gardens and trees. The quiet, green edges enclosed a mad world. Crossing streets, even at pedestrian walk-ways, struck terror to the heart. Life and limb seemed of small importance in the breathless heart of the gigantic, sprawling city. The only pleasant memory we carried away was of the Spanish ballet.

We had no intention of returning, but circumstances took us there and we landed in the city just in time for the great Mexican earthquake of 1985.

Why were we destined to walk into the middle of a big earthquake in a city that we did not love? Was it, perhaps, because of our lack of love? Sai Baba teaches that we must learn to love *all* people, all our brothers and sisters wherever they may be.

Our reason for returning was mundane enough. Tempted by high interest rates, we had invested money in a Mexican bank while still living in America with Walter and Elsie Cowan, who also had investments in Mexico. Believing in their financial sagacity, we followed suit. We transferred money from a good American bank where it accumulated as the result of some writing I had done for the American market. That was back in 1971. It was still holding its value against the American dollar and earning good interest when we visited Mexico City in 1975. I had a vague inner warning then about the safety of our investment, but I ignored it. Ten years later, our capital in Mexican currency plummeted to only a tenth of its value in American dollars at the time of investment. Furthermore, the money could not be taken out of the county. Rather than let it fade away to nothing, we decided to go there and spend the money on things we needed. We included Mexico in our 1985 trip around the world.   Arriving by air in Mexico City, we lost no time withdrawing our money from the bank and visiting some big department stores. But before we got far in the shopping program, we felt we must attend to two important things. One was to make contact with a couple we had met in Prashanti Nilayam in India -- Luis and Gail Muniz. They ran one of the few vegetarian restaurants in Mexico City. In addition, they had a book shop and publishing business. Years earlier, they had published a Spanish edition of my first book on Sai Baba, *Man of Miracles.* Their son, young Luis, was at that time a student in Sai Baba's university college at Prashanti Nilayam. We could not miss the opportunity of calling on them.

But the other matter was even more urgent. Our hotel, booked by a travel agent, was unsuitable; we wanted to find one closer to the heart of the city. After looking at several in the vicinity of the Pasea de la Reforma, we finally found one that seemed to call us. We stood on the grass verge under the trees, with the six lines of never-ending traffic roaring behind us, and looked across the cobbled, old-world street that ran along the front of the buildings. Nestled among the tall, many-storied structures of metal and masonry was one modest little hotel. It was only four stories high and looked as though it had been built when quality counted more than show. Its old-world air appealed to both Iris and me. But we knew from our last visit that the traffic noise would rage far into the night. "Perhaps they will have a quiet room at the back of the hotel, " Iris said. So we crossed the narrow cobbled street and went inside. The entrance foyer looked peaceful and inviting, with several armchairs and well-tended potted plants. On the wall hung an oil painting of a Spanish general; in a prominent position stood a life-sized statue of St Francis-- not the Assisi saint, we learned later, but one I had never heard of, from Spain. At the reception desk, a dignified gentleman greeted us; he seemed the personification of Spanish courtesy. He said he could give us a quiet suite on the third floor, rear.

We moved in before setting out to find the vegetarian restaurant owned by our Sai friends. It lay just far enough off the great avenue to be quiet. Very surprised to see us, Gail Muniz, director of the restaurant, greeted us warmly and we had a delightful lunch. She said her husband Luis was in another part of Mexico on business. We already knew her son Luis was in India; her daughter was at home with Gail. After lunch she drove us to see their book store and publishing business. I was surprised to see triple parking along the pavement in front of the shop. Gail calmly parked her car in the third line. "How do the cars on the inside get out?" I asked. "Oh, somehow," she replied, waving her arm with cool indifference as she led us into the book shop.

Gail offered to drive us the following evening to a meeting of the Mexico City Sai Baba Center. We accepted readily. We were eager to meet as many Mexican Sai devotees as possible. She also offered to drive us back to our hotel, but we preferred to walk. We wanted to look in the shops and perhaps make some of our purchases along the way.

We bought an item or two and returned to our hotel in the late afternoon. Determined to attack the job of spending our Mexican money wisely in the short time left to us, we decided to turn in early so we could get a fresh start shopping the next morning,

But that was not to be.

Our room was actually a combination bed-sitting room with a shower and dressing room attached. The next morning's early sun shone into the shower window while I took my turn at bathing. I stood relishing the way the sparkling water felt as it fell on me. All at once, the walls seemed to sway. Good heavens! Am I getting vertigo? I thought. Then I heard the sound of wall tiles falling in the dressing room next door. Next the shower tiles began to slide off the wall and crackle to the floor. Iris called urgently from the bed-sitting room, confirming my growing suspicion. "An earthquake!" she called, "Come out quickly!" Grabbing my towel, I dried hastily and joined Iris. By now the walls swayed dangerously.

Armed with our experience in the bombing raids on England during World War II, we quickly carried a couch across the swaying floor and put it under a huge, exposed beam that crossed the ceiling from one side of the room to the other. We sat down on it and watched as the ceiling and walls moved. We felt as if we were birds on the branch of a tree in a very strong wind. We could hear window glass breaking and crashing to the floor; simultaneously, big patches of plaster fell from the ceiling and walls and covered the floor with debris. Fortunately, none of the falling debris hit us. We thought the strong beam would hold unless the quake grew strong enough to take the building down. Putting our trust in God, we sat there and continually repeated the mantra "Om Sai Ram."

We had been in an earthquake once before, while sleeping in a lightly built garden house at the Cowan's residence in Tustin. But that quake was weaker -- six and a fraction on the Richter scale. As we heard great buildings crashing to the ground around our small hotel, we knew this one was much stronger, much more devastating.

We remembered England during the bombing raids of the blitzkrieg in the early part of World War II. In those raids, you were either hit by a bomb and suffered the damage, or you heard the bombers departing and knew it was over. There was no threat of a swaying building -- with the awful tension of expecting it to come down on you at any moment. The moment seemed to go on and on as we prayed that Mother Earth would cease her terrible shaking.

Mother Earth took her sweet time, but perhaps as time is measured, it was not so long. The big beam held but the room was a wreck when at last the swaying stopped. We thanked God, threw a kiss to the big beam above us and found that, mercifully, we could still boil some water to make a pot of tea. We drank it before getting dressed and going into the corridor. The door to the room opposite ours stood open; covering the bed was a big hunk of the ceiling. We knew that a young man from Cairo occupied the room, so we went in to see if he was all right. The bed had been slept in, but he was nowhere to be found.

We picked our way along a corridor strewn with broken plaster and down a stairway littered with rubble. Naturally, the elevator was not working. Except for shattered glass of the front door and windows, the foyer seemed practically unaffected. St. Francis still stood in his place on the floor; the Spanish general still hung on the wall. Now, the armchairs were all occupied. People milled about, the largest number in front of the reception desk. All eagerly waited their turn to settle accounts and move out of the hotel -- and out of Mexico City -- as fast as possible. We were relieved to see the young Egyptian alive and well. He came toward us speaking excitedly. "Jesus saved me! Jesus saved me!" "I'm glad," I replied. "But how?" "Early this morning he gave me an inner warning," said the young man. "I got up, dressed and came down to the foyer before the earthquake hit. I went outside and stood on the lawn under the trees, watching the buildings around me tumble down. Our hotel swayed a lot but did not fall." I said, "It threw a large part of the ceiling onto your bed. We saw that. What are you planning to do now?" His reply was immediate: "As soon as I can get a taxi, I'll go to the airport. If I can't get a plane to Egypt, I'll go anywhere -- provided it's away from Mexico City."

The rest of the people in the hotel seemed to have the same thought. Everyone wanted to get away from the city. If there were not enough planes to take them, they would sleep on the floor at the airport until a seat became available -- to anywhere.

When the crowd cleared from the reception desk, Iris and I approached it. The dignified Spaniard we had seen the day before had lost much of his dignity. His face was haggard, his eyes bloodshot. "Thank God our staunch little hotel has survived," I greeted him. He gave me a wan smile. "St. Francis has saved it so far," he said, "but there's sure to be another shock." Then, looking at his papers, he added, "You have paid for tonight as well." "Yes," I said, "We want to stay. We're booked on a plane to New York tomorrow." "Stay tonight!" he exclaimed in surprise, tinged with horror. "Everyone else has gone. It won't be safe to stay here any longer. The hotel will refund your money." "No," I said. "We will stay. I think it's as safe as anywhere in the city, much better than sleeping at the crowded airport. Besides, there may not be a second shock." He made further protests, but since we were determined, he said, "You'll have to sign a document saying you won't hold the hotel responsible for any damage that befalls you." We agreed, knowing that in any case we could not hold the hotel responsible for anything we suffered in an earthquake.

Then he sent an assistant to ask the hotel manager, Marta, to come out and help him. Perhaps he thought she would be able to convince us we should leave at once. Marta proved to be an attractive young woman, short in stature, with dark hair and eyes, rather pale skin and a very good command of English. She listened for a while to what the head receptionist had to say. Then, looking at us, she announced very firmly, "Mr. and Mrs. Murphet can stay if they wish. They do not need to sign any document. Move them down, if they agree, to a suite on the first floor facing front -- the one that has the least damage." She gave us a friendly smile and left.

The suite to which we moved was relatively undamaged. A patch of plaster had fallen from one wall; all the glass was out of the windows and the glass door that opened onto a little balcony overlooking the Pasea de la Reforma. It was a luxurious suite and we knew there would be no traffic on the great avenue to disturb our rest. We were glad to be there.

As we expected, the central boulevard of Mexico City was as silent as the grave. Well, almost. At rare intervals the whine of an ambulance or fire engine sounded. Iris always carried our breakfast necessities with us, so we fortified ourselves with a good meal, then went out to see what was left of the stricken city.

Along the Pasea de la Reforma, many of the proud, multi-storied, glittering buildings of yesterday were nothing more than a huge heap of rubble. In some, jagged pieces of wall stood up like giant teeth. We feared that thousands of people lay buried under the great hills of broken debris. Eventually, we reached the street that led off the avenue to Gail's vegetarian restaurant -- still standing, we were relieved to see, but closed. We knocked on the front door but nobody replied. After considerable knocking, we concluded that the place was empty. We headed back to our hotel to phone Gail. She could have been hurt -- or even killed -- in the quake.

We reached main avenue and hailed a bus going in our direction. It immediately stopped for us, even though we were nowhere near a bus stop. The other passengers smiled at us as we got on, as if we were members of their family. We offered our fare to the conductor but he smiled and shook his head, "No, the bus is free today." Everyone was so friendly, so warm and loving, that instead of getting off at our hotel, we continued on as far as the bus could go. Its route was eventually blocked by rubble. We had traveled a long way and most of the people had left the bus. We were the only two left when it turned to go back the same way it had come. We picked up more people on the return journey and saw that they, too, seemed to have been transformed. It was as if in the broken heart of their city, they had found their own heart center, making them one with all people.

As we viewed the heavily damaged city, we thought of those dead and badly hurt who lay under the wreckage of the gigantic buildings. We felt a oneness with all that remained alive, as if we could hug them to our hearts. Why does it take a disaster, we asked each other, to turn hatred into love, to make us see strangers as our own brothers and sisters, as Swami teaches us?

Back at the hotel, after some difficulty, we got a telephone line through to Gail's residence. She and her daughter were okay, she said. The restaurant was not open because supplies from the country could not get into the broken city. The Sai Baba meeting, scheduled for that evening, had been cancelled because all the members were engaged in Sai's service. "That sounds good," I replied. "What are they doing?" "Helping to get people out from under the rubble," she replied, "Afterward, they tend them, give them hot drinks and take the badly injured to hospitals." "Swami will approve of that," I said. "I hope your son will not get too much of a shock when he reads about the earthquake in the press." Gail's voice sounded worried as she replied." "Don't you think Swami may have seen the earthquake and told him we are all right?" Then I heard Iris' voice come through from the other extension. "I'm sure he will, Gail. Your son will know you are fine long before any press report reaches him. Swami will tell him." "Thank you," replied Gail, then went on. "My husband got through on the phone this morning. He will come back tomorrow."

As expected, any shops still standing were closed. Our shopping spree was off. How would we get lunch, we wondered. We walked and walked along many deserted streets, many with debris blocking our pathway. Footsore and weary, we headed back toward the hotel. Within a few blocks, we found one little restaurant that was offering meals. We sat down at a small table and ordered a vegetarian salad. It tasted like food for the gods. Afterward, we ate a very satisfying desert.

Thus, two refreshed and refuelled bodies arrived back at the hotel. The head receptionist looked at us with sad eyes, as if he thought we were mad to be still in his hotel. Another man spoke to him; he introduced the stranger as his brother, saying he was a taxi driver. We took the opportunity to book his taxi for our trip to the airport early next morning. The receptionist looked satisfied, as if this were the first spark of sanity we had shown.

"So, you think there will be another shock," I remarked to the two men. "Yes," they replied. "And this time," the receptionist went on, "Our hotel may not survive." "Don't you think St. Francis will hold it up?" I asked. He made no reply to that, but simply said, "The second shock could come at any time." His brother said, "If you would like to go to the airport now, I can still find a way through. But after another shock, who knows?" "It will be very crowded and uncomfortable to sleep at the airport," I responded. "I think we will trust to St. Francis."

We left them to walk upstairs to our suite. We rested on two easy chairs, looking through the shattered windows towards the great empty avenue. An eerie silence lay everywhere, as if the city held its breath, waiting for an even more devastating event. "I wonder how long we have to wait for the expected second shock?" asked Iris. "Just don't expect it at all," I replied. "It may never come. As Swami says, live in the moment and be happy whatever the circumstances." Iris said, "The city looks as if it were a terrible earthquake. I wonder what it measured on the Richter scale?" "We'll find out -- if we live," I replied. "If we don't, the measurement won't matter to us." We learned later that the Mexico City earthquake measured 8.1 on the Richter scale -- among the biggest on record. (A geologist friend told me that the largest quakes recorded were in the early 1960's, one in Chile and one in Alaska; both measured 9.0 on the Richter scale.

Iris offered to read aloud from a book we had been enjoying

together, but I felt like taking my usual siesta and was soon fast asleep. I was awakened by the scream of an ambulance careering along the avenue outside.

Iris, preparing supper from our travelling food stock, said, "We should get to bed early since the taxi will call for us in the morning at an ungodly hour." It was not quite dark when we climbed into the very comfortable bed. Looking up at the ceiling, I noted that this room also had a stout exposed beam across its center -- but I trusted we would not need it.

Scarcely had the thought left my mind when the bed began to sway. The second shock had begun. We jumped out of bed and again pulled a couch under the big beam. For the second time, we watched the walls lurch from side to side in the dim light through our large broken windows. With prayers to the Divine One, we began our mantra, "Om Sai Ram," aloud. We heard plaster fall to the floor, coming from the ceiling and the walls. What glass had remained in the windows and door fell with a noisy clatter but, though the floor under us moved, the couch stayed in place under the great beam. We heard noises outside the window that sounded as if everything left standing from the morning was now crashing into heaps on the ground.

I don't know how long the shock lasted, but it seemed a bit shorter than the first; but this time we heard more noise close to the hotel. When it was over, our room still intact, we thanked God for his protection. Then we explored around the suite. The flask of iced drinking water still stood and we each drank a tumbler full. Iris remarked, "I felt very nervous about the threatened second shock. I'm very relieved that it has come and gone. Do you think there might be another one tonight?" "No," I replied definitely. "Let's get to bed." But we heard a voice, soft but clear, calling our names outside the window. "Mr. and Mrs. Murphet," the voice said. "Please come downstairs and out the front door. Come quickly!" The voice had a pleading tone. It began anew and sounded urgent. "Come as quickly as you can, Mr. and Mrs. Murphet! We must tell you something."

Putting on our dressing gowns and slippers, we made our way down the stairs and through the front door. By now it was quite dark, but some street lights revealed a shadowy group of people standing under a tree on the narrow strip of lawn across the cobbled street in front of the hotel. "Thank God, you have come!" said Marta, and some of the others echoed her sounds of relief and welcome. In the group, I recognized our Spanish head receptionist and other members of the staff whom we did not know by name. Marta introduced a tall young man in his early twenties as the son of the chief director of the hotel. She explained why they had called us. The police had condemned the hotel, saying that no one could stay there as it could fall at any moment. Apparently it had been hit by the adjacent building. The police had already put a rope barrier across the front of the hotel. "We will find you accommodations for the night at some safer place. Two of our staff have already gone to look for it. And, of course, we will pay for it since you've already paid." This all seemed very drastic. We explained that we had to go back and gather our belongings. "No, you can't go in there," said Marta. "The police have forbidden it." "All our belongings, our money and our air tickets are up there," I said, "We need to collect them." But the others joined Marta in the protest, forbidding us to go. We insisted that we must take the risk. When they found that we were determined, Marta said, "Just one of you go; the other stay here." But that didn't suit our way of thinking at all.

Marta finally conceded that we could go if a policeman went with us. We had no objection to that suggestion. The young policeman who accompanied us was very pleasant and helpful. He assisted us in our packing, then carried our bags downstairs in front of us. When we came across the cobbled streets to the waiting group, we saw expressions of relief and welcome. We felt cared for, as if we were beloved members of their family.

We stood in our night attire, luggage beside us, and faced the little hotel which was expected to come tumbling down at any moment. Marta stood between Iris and me. We could see that she was trembling like a leaf; the strain of the quake's second shock and the threat to the hotel had been too much for her. We each put an arm around her and held her close. "Don't worry," I assured her, "The hotel will not fall." "But the police say it will," she replied, her voice quivering. "It will not fall," I assured her firmly. "Sai Baba will not let it fall." She had lost faith in St. Francis and probably had no idea who Sai Baba was, but she clung to the hope of help from a great magician. She repeated after me several times. "Sai Baba will not, will not let the hotel fall." After a time her trembling ceased.

The two scouts returned, saying they had found a room for us in an hotel further up the avenue; it had somehow withstood the earthquake and had not been condemned. Some staff members carried our bags along the road as Iris and I followed. We felt strange walking along the great Pasea de la Reforma in the middle of the night in slippers and dressing gowns, but no one else was abroad to see us. Eventually we were led through the door of a large, solid-looking hotel. It must have been very strongly built to have withstood the violent shaking that had destroyed so many other buildings. We entered a large foyer and saw that practically every inch of the floor was covered with sleeping bodies. Perhaps they had thought it safer down here than in their rooms; or perhaps other homeless people like us had found their way here. At the reception desk, a man and woman, smoking cigarettes nervously, greeted us, "Welcome, welcome!" We felt like heroes returning from some dangerous expedition.

We were guided up a flight of stairs into the first room in the corridor facing front. We guessed that patrons had deserted their rooms in favor of the floor of the great foyer. We climbed into very comfortable twin beds and I, for one, went straight to sleep.

Day was just breaking when we awoke. "I'm going to walk back to our little condemned hotel," I told Iris. "I want to see if it is still standing -- as I believe it will be." I left her to pack for our journey while I walked back along the side of the great avenue. As I had anticipated, our brave little hotel still stood staunchly, its forbidding rope barrier in front. I stepped over the barricade and walked to the front door. Through the gap left by broken glass, I called into the empty foyer, "Is anybody there?" My voice echoed through the emptiness of the hotel. Feeling happy that my faith and prophesy had proved true, I walked back along the avenue. I began to wonder if I would be able to find a taxi to the airport. I mentally asked Sai Baba's help in this.

When I neared the hotel where Iris was waiting, I saw a man standing next to his taxi on the cobbled street. I asked if he would take us to the airport. He agreed and waited in front of the hotel while I went upstairs to get Iris. She had a cup of tea waiting for me. There was no time for breakfast so I gratefully drank the tea and carried our luggage downstairs.

The sun was rising on the scene of desolation as we drove slowly, making many detours to avoid blockages caused by fallen buildings. We talked sympathetically with the driver. We felt as one with the people in their great suffering. We did not tell him that formerly we had not liked the people of his big city, but we let him know that we liked them now, felt very close to them and prayed that the grace of God would help them recover from the disaster. He told us the fate of many fallen buildings as we drove along.

We arrived at the airport and I reached for my wallet, realizing that he could charge me anything he liked; instead, I found his fare very modest indeed. It seemed no more than what we would have paid had we had come directly from the hotel with no detours. Saying goodbye, he kissed Iris' hand. He and I shook hands and I noticed that his eyes were filled with tears. I knew he had been touched by our sincere feelings for his broken city and its people.

We expected a long wait at the airport for our plane to New York, but in less than an hour we were winging over the tragic capital of Mexico.

What a pity, I thought, that it takes a great disaster to bring us to the truth of what Sai Baba teaches: that not only are we one with God, but we are one with every other being because God is in all -- and indeed the reality of all. I remembered that I had felt the same experience forty-five years earlier when the enemy bombs were shattering London. The Londoners are normally class- conscious and cold to each other, but under the hammering of the bombs, they became as one united family. How difficult it seems under normal conditions to feel love for all mankind. Yet on the spiritual path, that is exactly what we must learn to do.

I close the chapter with two items that brought us good cheer and joy on the last stage of our journey.

When we arrived in London, we found that the restriction on the exportation of Mexican money had been lifted. Instead of the money we brought from Mexico being valueless, we were able to use it in London.   Arriving at our last port of call, Prashanti Nilayam in India, we heard that with his omnipresence, our Lord Sai had witnessed the earthquake in Mexico City and when it was over, he called his college student, Luis Muniz, and told him of the event, assuring him that no member of his family had come to any harm. He added that no Sai Baba devotee in Mexico City at that time had been hurt at all.   We should, of course, have known this without being told, but it did our hearts good to hear it confirmed by Swami himself.

When disasters come upon us -- as they inevitably will in this imperfect world --the grace and protection of God himself is a great boon. This is one of several important spiritual lessons we learned in our journey through the great earthquake.

13

A DISTINGUISHED SCHOLAR AND DEVOTEE

I first saw him walking alone in the garden of Brindavan, Sathya Sai Baba's ashram near Whitefield. He was a balding man with a broad, prominent forehead that seemed to weight his head forward as he walked. He seemed to be in deep thought, far away from his immediate surroundings. Although the day was quite warm, he had a thick woollen scarf wound round his neck with the ends hanging forward. He also wore a loose-fitting jacket of ancient vintage, I thought, and his trousers were a little too short -- above his ankles. He made me think of an absent-minded professor, probably from a university of the western world. As I stood with my wife, Iris, watching this lone figure move about the garden, I had no idea who he was and even less idea that he was to become my much-loved spiritual brother.

We were staying with Sai Baba in his big two-story Brindavan house and it was not yet the time of day when a crowd would start gathering for Swami's *darshan* and *bhajan* singing in the area of the ashram beyond the gate of his private garden. Presently Sai Baba himself came out of his front door and stood with us in his portico. The stranger came toward us through the arches of the covered walkway. When the man reached the portico, Swami introduced him as Dr. V.K. Gokak, vice-chancellor of Bangalore University. I had never met a person so high in the academic world and I was a little surprised and impressed by his smiling, warm, friendly manner. The humility of wisdom rather than the pride of learning seemed to be his keynote. Swami left us together. Iris went inside to attend to some domestic chore. Dr. Gokak and I sat down on the nearest garden seat to talk.

I found that he was quite a new boy in the crowd, which was multiplying swiftly around Sathya Sai Baba at that time. Since Dr. Gokak was vice-chancellor of Bangalore University between 1966 and 1969, our meeting occurred then -- probably toward the middle of that period.

Gokak was in the habit of driving out frequently from Bangalore to see Sai Baba and would often stay for a while after the interview to give me the benefit of his congenial company. That was when I learned the story of how he came to Swami and some details of his interesting background.

He did not tell me much about his academic career, but I heard more about that later from others. I soon found, however, that he and I were one in our great love of English literature. He had originally been a follower of Sri Aurobindo, who had a deeply philosophical mind. Like Dr Gokak himself, Aurobindo, in his lifetime, had been a literary man and a poet. Both men had been molded to different degrees by the academic life of England. Though Gokak's contact with Aurobindo had been mainly through his writings, he knew Mother Mira personally and had accepted her as his spiritual leader after the death of Aurobindo. For a period before Gokak came to Sai Baba, the Pondicherry Mother had, at his request, tried to heal his daughter of some mysterious disease, the understanding of which had eluded orthodox medicine. Mother Mira knew what the trouble was but could make no progress in healing it. Gokak told me she had said, "Your daughter is hanging onto the entity. She just will not let it go." So Gokak understood that she had a psychical, rather than a physical, problem. He sensed that any run-of-the-mill psychiatrist would probably resort to drug therapy. He did not want this.

Having heard of the divine healing powers that Sai Baba often demonstrated, he decided to take his daughter to the great *Avatar*. But, in keeping with the traditional etiquette of Indians in such matters, he would not do so without his guru's permission. So he asked Mother Mira. She replied that he was quite free to do whatever he wished. Gokak began to take his daughter and his wife to see Swami whenever possible. They received the grace of frequent interviews with Sai Baba. I feel that perhaps two major reasons for Swami's close attention to the family were, first, his compassion for the sick daughter; and also his foreknowledge that the eminent scholar and educator, Gokak, would become an eminent Sai devotee.

Several times during interviews, Mrs. Gokak invited Swami to their house in Bangalore for dinner. Swami just smiled sweetly at the invitations and said nothing. Eventually, Mrs. Gokak asked Swami why he wouldn't come. His reply seemed mysterious. "I will come when Gokak wants me," he said. The vice-chancellor was present and protested strongly that he **did** want Swami to come, but again Swami smiled silently.

Though the health of the Gokak's daughter seemed to be improving, she was far from cured. No doubt, Swami knew her destiny but he did not tell her parents. According to Mother Mira, the entity the girl was so strongly attached to -- and, therefore, wouldn't let go -- was a very dear friend on the other side of that thin line which divides the living from the so-called dead. Whatever the reason, the pull on the other side of the line was so strong that eventually she passed away.

Meanwhile, Dr. Gokak's love for Swami grew stronger and stronger. In reminiscing about this period, he told me that in his shrine room at home Mother Mira held the pride of place, although several other divine forms graced the altar. A small photo of Sathya Sai Baba hung on the wall.

One day he felt moved to take the photo and place it on the altar. The following day, when Gokak and his wife were having an interview with Swami, Swami said, "I will be pleased to come to your place for dinner when next you ask me." Delighted, Mrs. Gokak immediately invited him and a date was set. Gokak did not have to think much about this event to realize that by taking Swami's photo from the wall and giving it prominence on his shrine, he had given an outward and visible sign that he accepted Sathya Sai Baba as his sadguru. He realized, too -- as many others, including me, have come to understand -- that Swami knows what you do in your private home. Gokak later recalled something he had heard Swami say: "There is room for only one seat at the center of your heart."

One evening shortly afterwards, Swami went to dinner at the palatial house occupied by the university vice-chancellor during his term of office. Swami took Iris and me with him, to our great delight. On several occasions before, we had had the inestimable grace of going with Swami to meals at the homes of devotees. The houses he took us to varied from humble dwellings to the large homes of wealthy or eminent Sai devotees. Gokak's house was quite palatial; the room in which we dined was very large and stately. The meal followed the pattern we had come to know, as it was the one that prevailed at all the dinners we attended with Swami in Indian homes. The guests sat around the room, their backs to the wall; the luxurious oriental carpet stretched from corner to corner as their seat. Iris and I had grown accustomed to sitting cross-legged and eating food served on large leaf plates covering the carpet before us. Swami sat on a chair before a small table at one end of the room.

While several waiters brought pails of food to serve the guests, Mrs. Gokak herself served Sai Baba. She was both hostess and humble waitress to the one they knew as God. The host, Dr. Gokak, sat immediately to the right of Swami but, like his guests, he sat cross-legged on the floor. I cannot remember the names of all the dishes we had, but I do remember that the food was excellent. I understand now -- some thirty years later -- what I did not fully appreciate then: We were truly blessed to be with the Avatar at his invitation on such occasions.

During the months and years that followed our first meeting, I enjoyed many talks given by Gokak from Sai Baba's platform. He spoke clearly, the ring of devotion in his deep voice. The English he used was a joy to hear. Not surprisingly, his words and phrases were reminiscent of the writings of his first spiritual teacher, Sri Aurobindo. The great master of Pondicherry who had drunk deeply of English culture, was in a way a bridge between East and West. Dr. Gokak gave support to that literary bridge as he clothed the ancient, eternal wisdom of India in the beauty of the English tongue.

When Gokak's distinguished academic background had percolated slowly to me through the years, I found that I was right in my first impression of him that morning in the garden. He had looked to me like an absent-minded professor. He most certainly was a professor with many years experience, but I only knew him as absent-minded on one occasion -- which I shall relate later.

His tertiary education was distinguished by a Master of Arts degree, First Class, at Bombay University. While at Oxford in England, he obtained another M.A. degree in English literature at the top of his class. Later he received honorary doctorates in literature from two universities -- the University of South Pacific in California and Kanataka University in India. In 1931, when he was just twenty-two years old, he began his teaching career. Between then and 1966, when he became vice-chancellor of Bangalore University, Gokak held the chair in English literature at half a dozen universities in India, serving as college principal at most of them. By the time I met him in the garden at Brindavan, he had been a professor for about thirty-five years. Dr. Gokak was not only a leading educator, but also a prolific writer. He had written more than 50 books, some in English but the majority in his own language, Kanada.

His great love of literature formed a strong link between us, though the firmest link in our brotherhood was his deep love of Swami and a penetrating understanding of his teachings and mission. After he had become firmly established in doing Sai work, Gokak wrote a very enjoyable and enlightening book on Sai Baba.

Because of our close friendship, Gokak sometimes told me things he had gleaned from his close intercourse with Sai Baba -- especially those things he thought I might have particular interest in. He told me, for instance, that one day he remarked to Swami, "The people at Pondicherry say that Aurobindo was an Avatar, Swami. Is that so?" Swami replied, "Yes, he was an Avatar of the individual, whereas I am an Avatar for the masses." I found this quite interesting. With few exceptions, only those with a philosophical turn of mind find interest in the spiritual literature of the profound poetic pen of Sri Aurobindo, but everybody can imbibe with delight and satisfaction Swami's presentation of the timeless wisdom for which the ancient rishis laid the foundation.

During the happy years of my association with Dr Gokak, several events remain in my memory above the others. Despite our close friendship, I always called him "Doctor" and he always addressed me as "Mr Murphet." Looking back, this seems like a strange Dickensian courtesy between us, but it also sprang from our mutual respect. One incident I like to remember gave me insight into Swami that I would not otherwise have had. Swami had invited a number of leading poets from different parts of India to read one of their poems on his platform before a large assembly of devotees. He gave each one of them a jacket, or mantle, of a beautiful shade of blue, just right as a symbol of literary distinction. One of the readers was Dr Gokak. His was a short poem in English on the inspiring subject of the Sai Avatar. He told me later that while reading the poem, he glanced down at Sai Baba who was sitting on a chair at his side. He was surprised -- indeed, amazed! -- to see that Swami's eyes were filled with tears. At the first opportunity, he asked Swami the reason for this. Swami replied simply, "Because it was the truth." I, too, was surprised that the Avatar could be moved to tears by a verbal expression of deep truth. I thought of the lines of John Keats, "Beauty is truth, truth beauty -- that is all ye know on earth and all ye need to know."

Another event I find real joy in remembering is an interview Dr. Gokak and my wife and I had with Sai Baba. Although Swami usually spoke in English at such personal interviews, on this occasion he asked Gokak to come along with us as an interpreter. The interview was shortly after the visit of the "vibhuti baby" to Prashanti Nilayam ashram (*Footnote: for details of the event see my book *Sai Baba Avatar*.) Swami explained the deeper meaning of that event and went into some profound aspects of lessons to be learned along the Sai path of the spirit. Some of what he said was spoken in good simple English, but at other times, when plumbing the depths, he spoke in an Indian language that Gokak understood; he interpreted the words of the Avatar in his lucid English. Thus the journey we took with Sai Baba lay in some of the deepest regions in the ocean of truth. Swami seemed to disregard the passage of time; time vanished for me as well, so that when we finally emerged into the bright sunshine of the ashram and saw figures moving here and there, we felt we had emerged into a strangely different world. "Well," remarked Dr. Gokak, "that is the best interview I ever had." Iris and I felt the same way. My soul-relationship with the good doctor seemed even more firmly cemented than before.

When the Sathya Sai University was founded in 1981, Swami had two ex-vice-chancellors among his devotees. One was the eminent scientist, Dr. Bhagavantam, who, as well as having served at one time as scientific adviser to the government of India, had also been for a term vice-chancellor of the Osmania University at Hyderabad. The other was Dr. Gokak who, as mentioned earlier, held the post at Bangalore University. I was delighted when Sai Baba selected the open-hearted, broadly-cultured Dr V.K.Gokak to be the vice-chancellor of his own university. My friend served in this capacity from 1981 to 1985 -- double the normal time for such a position.

In 1983, during his term of office, an international Sai Baba Conference took place in Rome. I was selected to represent Australia at this conference, probably because, with my wife's help, I had established the first Sai Baba center in Australia. Iris and I took a plane to Italy about two weeks before the conference, spending time in Lugarno, Switzerland, with our Sai friends Mr. and Mrs. Wolk. We also visited the chief organizer of the conference, Antonio Craxi, at his home near Milan. We found that Craxi was exerting every effort to persuade Swami to go to the conference, but instead Swami sent his vice-chancellor,

Gokak. The scholarly devotee had also represented Sai Baba in
the United States when frequent invitations to Swami reached the
point of intensity when the compassionate Lord felt that
something should be done. Swami could not go himself, he often
said, until he got his own house -- India -- in order.

Of the inspiring International Conference in Rome, all I want to
include here are some observations that concern the subject of
this chapter: V.K. Gokak. Among the many talks given from the
platform at the conference, one stirring and memorable address
came from Sir George Trevelyan of England, a fine speaker with
many years of experience in adult spiritual education. But to me,
without a doubt, the most deeply moving discourses of the
conference were the two delivered by Dr. Gokak. But I was
alarmed that at the end of each, he was helped off the stage by
two men. Why? I wondered? Had his health deteriorated? He
had delivered his addresses with great strength and fervor. The
rule at the conference was that when anyone spoke from the stage
in English, there had to be an interpreter to translate the speech
into Italian for the benefit of the many non-English-speaking
Italians in the audience. In his final address, Gokak was so
caught up in his subject that he forgot to pause at intervals to let
the interpreter do his translation. Instead Gokak spoke straight on
from the beginning to the end of his speech. (Later, a written
translation was circulated among the Italian members.) When I
asked him later why he had to be helped from the platform at the
end of the addresses -- even though he walked to the podium in
the ordinary way at the beginning -- he replied, "I get so carried
away when I am talking for a long time about Swami that I am
unable to walk down the steps by myself. In my last talk I was so
transported out of normal awareness, I forgot all about pausing
for the interpreter. I am very sorry about that." I said, "We who
understand English enjoyed your spiritual eloquence all the more
for that. Chopping it up for frequent interpretation would have
spoiled it."

We were returning to India on the same plane and Gokak

suggested that we sit together to enjoy each other's company. I was pleased at his request, but in the end both of us slept most of the way. Our work at the conference in Rome had been quite strenuous.

In subsequent visits to Prashanti Nilayam in the latter years of the eighties, I usually found the good doctor there and we always happily renewed our association. I especially appreciated these times because I knew he spent most of his time at his home in Bangalore carrying on his creative writing, reaping many official honors and awards.

When Iris and I arrived at Prashanti Nilayam from Australia in September, 1992, I could find no sign of my friend. Thinking that he was probably working at his home in Bangalore, I decided to visit him there before leaving for home two months later. I asked a university official, a Sai devotee, if he knew of his whereabouts. The man replied in a quiet tone, "Professor Gokak died last April."

I had heard reports that he suffered from a rather serious type of diabetes, yet I was sadly shocked by the news of his death. I had lost a worthy Sai brother, but he had not lost his place in my heart.

I learned that two prominent Indian leaders paid tribute to Vaniaka Krishna Gokak in funeral orations. One, Sri P.V. Narasimha, Prime Minister of India, said, "He was a person who not only enriched literature, but also greatly enriched our lives. The sensitivity of his expression proved that man's creativity has no limits."

14

GODMEN AND MOTHERS

In his book *Easwarama,* on the life of the human mother of
Sathya Sai Baba, Professor N. Kasturi relates in his first chapter
how the great Godmen of ancient times were born of human, very
pure mothers without the aid of human fathers.   In some
mysterious manner, the conception was brought about by divine
intervention and divine entry into the womb. All Christians
know, for example, that this story is given in their scriptures
about the conception of Jesus. In the ordinary way, the human
species, like all animal species, require the junction of the male
and female for conception to take place. This is an accepted law
of Nature and laws of Nature, some would say, are God's laws
and cannot be broken. But are there deeper laws which supersede
the laws of Nature as we know them? Or are we dealing, not with
breaking the laws of Nature, but simply with myth? Isn't it true
that in stories surrounding events that happened thousands of
years ago, discrimination between legend and fact is difficult? It
seems strange, nevertheless, that, though details differ, the same
claim of supernatural conception is made concerning the birth of
Godmen.   Certainly, we cannot say that time, the great
legend-builder, plays a part in the story of a miraculous
conception that took place during our own era.

One day during the early years of his manhood, Sathya Sai
Baba was sitting in a room teaching a small group of his
followers. A learned pundit by the name of Ramasharma was in
the group. Also present was N. Kasturi, who tells the story, and
Sathy Sai's humble, modest little mother, Easwarama. I recall
from my own experience in the early years that Swami was
giving what might be called a parlor talk to a small group of
followers; at times, he paused to allow his listeners to ask
questions. During such a pause, the learned pundit asked what
the others thought was a rather strange question -- and one which
probably most of them did not understand. He asked, "Swami,

was your conception a *pravesa* or a *prasava*?" Swami, of course, understood the meaning of these two Sanskrit words and understood the intent of the question. Looking at his mother, he said, "Tell them about your experience at the well."

His mother, a very shy woman, did not enjoy speaking in public. But she had great respect for her God-man son, whom she always addressed as "Swami," after the revelation of his true identity when he was about fourteen years old. So, in a quiet, hesitant voice, she told the following story:

One day her mother-in-law told Easwarama that on the previous night she had a dream of Sathya Narayana -- the name given by Indians to man's inner god. (Incidentally, Easwarama and her mother-in-law had offered constant prayers and *pujas* to the god-form, Sathya Narayana, before the birth of Sathya Sai Baba. In honor of the god, they named the bright-eyed infant Sathya Narayana, which can be translated, "Truth, the inner divinity of man.") Her mother-in-law did not tell Easwarama the details of the dream, rather simply warned her not to be afraid if something very unexpected and unusual happened to her. The very next morning, something did happen. Easwarama stood by the well and looked about absent-mindedly before beginning to draw water. Her eyes fell on the rocky hills beyond the village and suddenly she saw a ball of blue light moving rapidly toward her. It drew closer; surely she would have panicked and fled had her mother-in-law warned her not to be afraid. So she stood still, simply opening her eyes wide in wonder as the gleaming, shining ball came within a few feet of her, then seemed to enter into her. As this was more than she could bear, she fainted and fell. Returning to consciousness, she awoke with a strange feeling. The feeling turned to joy as something deep within her told her she was pregnant. In the days to come, this proved to be true and in due time the smiling, curly-headed baby Sathya Narayana was born.

The complete silence that followed Easwarama's story was broken by Swami who said to the pundit, "There. You have your

answer. I was a *pravesa*, not a *prasava*. I was not begotten."
The word *pravesa* means a direct entry; *prasava* means a
conception brought about in the ordinary way -- that is, begotten
by a human father.

Kasturi and the others present in the room knew that Swami
meant that he -- in the form of a blue light -- had entered directly
into the womb of his earthly mother. We know, of course, that all
things are possible with God, but why would he bring about such
a conception?

Certainly not because there is anything wrong or shameful in
normal sexual activity between husband and wife. The function
is decreed by God himself so that the human race can multiply.
A story in the Hindu scriptures illustrates this. First, the story
goes, God created some highly advanced *rishis* of both sexes, but
they simply meditated and showed no signs of reproducing and
multiplying. God had to begin again. Why, then, is the human
father excluded -- as seems the case -- in the incarnation of
Godmen?

We can consider a few possible reasons. For a Godman to be
born in the usual way with a human body, he must have a human
mother.   But accounts of such epoch-making events as the
incarnations of the great Godmen, show that He goes to great
trouble to select the right mother. She must be pure of heart,
alike the innocent Devaki, mother of Krishna; Mary, mother of
Jesus; and Easwarama, mother of Sathya Sai Baba. She must
have little, or no, bad *karma*. Of course, such karma would not
be passed on to the pure divine being who came into her womb,
but it might have an effect on the body He built from the physical
material provided by the mother. The Godman must make sure,
in advance, that his physical body will not suffer from defects or
diseases inherited from the mother. Selecting such a well-nigh
perfect, pure-minded, spiritually holy woman at the appropriate
time for the great incarnation is no easy task. We should
remember too that the search is restricted to the country that God
has already decided is the best for his incarnation.   This is

usually, though not always, India, "the guru of the world."

The task of selection would be doubled in difficulty, at least, if a male partner of equal karma-free purity had to be found. So the omnipotent, divine being who created the polarity of the sexes is not himself a servant of that polarity. Having within his being the seeds of both male and female, he is able to fertilize the egg of the selected mother of the *Avatar* of God-to-be.

Apart from these humble speculations on the subject, there may be other deeper reasons beyond the understanding and knowledge of man for such miraculous conceptions. In witnessing the miracles of Sai Baba, I came to believe in the miracles of Jesus, about which there had hitherto been doubts in my mind. In like manner, the story of Sathya Sai Baba's direct entry into the womb of his mother, confirmed by him, leads me to give credence to the stories of other miraculous, sacred births, including that of Jesus the Christ.

There can be no doubt that these mighty beings who come to us from time to time, bearing the gifts of truth, love and peace, are very special indeed and liable to have special births. Furthermore, as all the evidence shows, they have a cherishing love for the holy mother. The Christian scriptures tell, for example, how from the cross Jesus gave his mother into the keeping of his beloved disciple, John. No doubt he was aware that her uncle, Joseph of Arimathea, who became the head of the family after the death of Joseph, the carpenter, would become Mary's protector. Apparently, the dying Jesus wanted her to have the very special care and comfort of his closest and most-loved disciple.

Accounts of what happened to the mother of Jesus after that first Easter vary and belong to legend rather than history. Yet, in the centuries since her life on earth, she has been the center of well-authenticated historic visions in various parts of Christendom; these have been an inspiration and help to the followers of Christ. Also, it is stated that, at the middle of this century, the head of the Roman Catholic Church announced that

Mary, the mother of Jesus, had been transported bodily to join the godhead along with the Father, Son and Holy Spirit. I assume that the term "bodily" means the glorified body, the same as that of Jesus at his resurrection. The outstanding psychologist, Carl Jung, stated at the time that the inculcation of femininity into the hitherto purely male godhead would bring a greater, and much needed, feminine influence into the worldly affairs of Christendom. This, he said, would be a great benefit to mankind and aid in our struggle towards the Golden Age. One can see signs of that in our modern times.

Sathya Sai Baba, arriving on earth some two millennia after the departure of Jesus, showed a similar tender, caring love for his mother, Easwarama. (Of interest is that the name Easwarama means the mother of the highest god-form, generally called Easwara by the Hindus.) Accounts of Sathya Sai Baba's early years -- at the time he began his spiritual mission -- suggest that largely to please his mother, he did not immediately take the ocher robe and leave home, as many spiritual leaders do, but established his ashram in the village where he was born, Puttaparthi. Moreover, for a number of years, he continued to wear white attire. After a few years, however, he established his ashram, Prashanti Nilayam (Abode of Great Peace) on the edge of his native village and began to wear the red-orange robe that now distinguishes him.

When I first went there in the early sixties, Easwarama could be seen every day moving about the grounds of Prashanti Nilayam. In appearance, she was unpretentious, modest, humble and withdrawn. She dressed in simple clothing, while her soft brown eyes, in a wrinkled face beneath copious grey hair, seemed remote, without much interest in the world around her. Her husband had died and her sole interest seemed to be her Godman son, whose spiritual kingdom was growing as she watched. I think even if I could have spoken her language, Telegu, I would have hesitated to break into what seemed a private, sacred silence. But my friend, A. Chakravati, retired Air Force squadron-leader and champion parachute jumper, used to talk to Easwarama whenever he visited the ashram. He and his wife would touch the old mother's feet in reverence and try in every way they could to please her.

On one occasion -- an important one as it turned out -- they invited her to come stay with them at their home in Varanasi on the Ganges. Since the old woman did not recognize the city by its modern name of Varanasi, they called it its ancient name of Kashi. When she realized that she was being invited to stay at Kashi, her eyes lit up and a smile of happiness came onto her serene but somber face. "Ah," she said, "I would love to go to Kashi. I have never been there." Then she continued regretfully, "But it's too far for me to go."

A few months later in Varanasi, Chakravati woke up early one morning to witness a strange sight. Swami and Easwarama, his mother, were walking across the bedroom, past the foot of his bed. Chakravati uttered an exclamation and woke his wife. They both sat up to watch Swami lead his mother by the arm. They could hear him say in a gentle voice, "Yes, this is Kashi." Then he took her through the wall and out of the room. Both figures looked very real. Chakravati knew they must be in their subtle bodies. Both he and his wife had a feeling that Easwarama had died and was moving in her astral body.

Later, news from Prashanti Nilayam confirmed their suspicion; Easwarama had died about that time. It seemed evident that Swami was showing his mother Varanasi after her death; perhaps he took her through the room of Chakravati and his wife because they had invited her there and she had expressed her longing to them to visit. Swami, unable, because of his busy program, to take his mother to the sacred city on the Ganges during her lifetime, took her there -- in his great love and compassion -- after her death, in order to fulfil the sacred desire of her deep heart's core.

This, to me, is a measure of the deep, loving care and solicitude that a Godman feels for his earthly mother.

15

THE REMARKABLE STORY OF DR. BHATIA

In the early days at Prashanti Nilayam ashram, I was puzzled by the fact that most people spoke of Sai Baba as an *Avatar* of Siva, whereas the Hindu religion states that the early great Avatars, such as Rama and Krishna, were incarnations of Vishnu. One day when I asked Swami about this, he said, "There is only one God." I said no more but contemplated a great deal on the question. I know there is but one God and that what is called the *Trimurti* -- that is, Brahma, Vishnu and Siva -- may manifest as separate forms although they are only facets of the one Being. The one Being, when without form, is known as Brahman; when *with* form, it is generally called Easwara. So it seemed to me that, though Sai Baba is an Avatar of the one God, he manifests the facet of Siva much more than the other two facets, Brahma and Vishnu.

Each of the three God forms of the Trimurti has a consort who, although in the deepest sense is an aspect of God, also manifests as a separate female form. The consort of Siva, for example, is known generally as Parvati, although she has other names depending on the function she performs. When merged with Siva as his feminine aspect, she is known as Shakti.

During his former life at Shirdi village, Sai Baba was considered to be mainly an incarnation of the Siva facet, with very little of his feminine -- or Shakti -- aspect in evidence; but in his present form of Sathya Sai Baba, he is considered to be a good balance of the male and female aspects, or a union of Siva and Shakti. To put it another way, both Siva and his consort, Parvati, seem to be merged in our Swami, Sathya Sai Baba.

I hope these introductory remarks will help people unfamiliar with the Hindu religion better understand the subject of this chapter -- Dr. Bhatia's remarkable story.

The story begins in October, 1993, when Sai Baba told Dr. Naresh Bhatia to spend a month in America. The official purpose of this journey was for Dr. Bhatia, who was in charge of the blood bank at Sai Baba's world famous hospital near his ashram, to attend an international conference on blood banks. While in America, he was to visit a number of hospitals and to learn anything he could about this important aspect of the medical profession. The American conference was due to start on October 23; on October 20, the pale-skinned young doctor with soft, black eyes made his way to the office of the American Consul in Madras to obtain his visa.

"I had been told," he relates, "that the American Consulate is very cautious about issuing visas to Indian doctors. They apparently fear that they may stay in America. But I didn't worry. I knew if Swami wanted me to go, nothing could stop me. And if Swami didn't want me to go, nothing could make me.

"I saw a nice-looking young American woman sitting at the desk and I greeted her with, 'Hello, sister.' She looked at me as if to say, 'Who is this fellow calling me sister?' She looked at my papers and asked, 'Dr.. Bhatia, how long have you been working in Sai Baba's hospital?' 'Since its inception,' I replied, 'in November, 1991.' Then she asked another question, 'How long have you been a devotee of Sai Baba?' I replied, 'In 1970, when I was a first-year medical student in the Punjab, I happened to read Howard Murphet's book, *Sai Baba, Man of Miracles*. Since then I have had a great deal of love for Sai Baba and faith in him.' Then she asked, 'What do you do for Sai Baba?' 'I love him and serve him.' 'How?' 'I serve him by serving other people.' She seemed to want to know more, so I told her about Swami's beautiful hospital, which I think of and call a temple of healing, rather than a hospital. 'Well,' she said, 'I don't believe there is any such hospital that can give you free treatment.' 'Sister,' I said, 'I invite you to come and see for yourself and experience the temple of healing that God has created.' After that she just signed the paper, giving me the visa for America.

"I heard later that she had refused two or three people just before I arrived. I was now free to fly from Madras to Dubai, from there to England, and finally from England to New York. Having emphasized to the airline that I was a non-smoker and strict vegetarian, I was amazed and extremely disappointed to find myself seated in the smoking section, surrounded by smoking passengers. The air became quite suffocating, but I just kept quiet and prayed to Swami: 'Swami, you promised to bless me and be with me and take care of me, but you have let them put me here.' Then suddenly I forgot all about the choking tobacco smoke, because I saw Swami himself walk up and sit in the empty seat beside me. He held my hand and I was in such a state of bliss that I was unconscious of my surroundings until we circled to land at Dubai."

"Doctor," I said, interrupting his story. "He held your hand, you say. Did his hand seem like solid flesh?" "Oh, yes," he replied, "warm and firm like any human hand." So, I thought, he must have been in his subtle body to come into the plane after it was in the air; then he materialized himself, or at least the hand Dr Bhatia was holding, to physical matter. I have heard other stories in which he has done this. Swami apparently did not continue sitting in the seat during the forty-five minutes stop-over at Dubai. Most of the passengers got off the plane, but Dr. Bhatia remained in his seat, still in a state of bliss, thanking Swami for transforming what could have been a horrible journey into a journey of great joy. Soon they took off on the next leg of the journey from Dubai to London. Dr. Bhatia continues:

"In the seat Swami had occupied, now sat a big man who immediately took out a fat cigar, lit it and began puffing smoke in my face. Suddenly an announcement came over the intercom stating that a jacket and a book had been found. The voice said that an attendant would bring them around so the owner could claim them. The jacket was brought first, then the book. I saw that the title of the book was *Sai Baba, the Ultimate Experience*, written by Phyllis Krystal. Tears sprang to my eyes and I said under my breath, 'Swami!' Then Swami seemed to speak from the book, saying, 'Don't worry, I am around you. I am in all parts of the plane, taking care of you, so don't worry.' I called to the hostess who was carrying the book and said, 'Sister, I am Dr. Bhatia and I work in Sai Baba's hospital. If nobody claims the book, I have a devotional attachment to it. Please don't throw it away, but give it to me if nobody claims it, if you will.' She agreed. But both the jacket and the book belonged to a woman travelling in first class. The gentleman sitting next to me put out his cigar and said, 'You're a doctor, working in Sai Baba's hospital? I'm from Sri Lanka but I work in London. I'm also a doctor.' He said his aunt suffered from heart trouble and asked if I thought she could be admitted to Sai Baba's hospital. I told him to ask his aunt to write me and I would arrange for a check-up. I added that treatment at the hospital was free. We spent the rest of the journey to London talking about Sai Baba's hospital and his teachings. The man forgot about his cigar and I was so completely absorbed in talking about Swami that I was not troubled by any other tobacco smoke. In this way, Swami took care of me from Dubai to London."

After landing at Heathrow, Bhatia had to travel to another airport to take a plane to New York. He describes what happened when he presented his boarding pass to the woman at the desk:

"She asked to see my passport, then looked hard at my passport photo, then at my face, again at the passport and again at my face. I began to panic. I thought my trip had been cancelled for some reason. What would I do here? I thought. I knew nobody. I had nowhere to go. Then the woman said, 'Dr. Bhatia, British Airways is pleased to upgrade you from economy class to executive business class. You are a guest of British Airways.' 'But, Sister,' I said, 'who does me this honor?' 'I don't know. The instructions were sent to me by high officials.' They took me to the executive business class and seated me just behind the cockpit. It was very comfortable -- and in a non-smoking zone. Then a gentleman came and said, 'Dr. Bhatia, we have good news. What time would you like dinner?' 'Any time,' I replied. 'We have Indian food for you,' he said and brought a meal with all the Indian dishes I like most. Even my wife had never given me **all** my favorite foods at one time.

"At the New York airport, my hosts greeted me with love, which I knew came through them from Swami, for they were Sai devotees. The entire time I spent in America, I was surrounded by love from Swami. When I went from hospital to hospital, talking to people in blood banks, most of them wanted to know about Swami, of his teachings and his great hospital. They openly expressed their wishes, saying, 'Anytime you need our services, please let us know. We will go there to work.' I replied, 'I am not the person to arrange this for you, but any time Swami wants you, you will be there, without my asking him.' I felt the Lord around me all the time and my visit in America passed with great joy and with many interesting happenings. One of them I would like to relate:

"I was invited to a Sai Baba meeting in a private house in Miami. The woman who owned the house and led very good Sai Baba meetings there, was named Mrs. Bettina Biggart.. An old devotee of Sai Baba, she first met him in 1964. She also seemed to think that all her countrymen were loquacious and long-winded, whenever they got onto a public platform. I knew I was expected to speak, but I was dumbfounded when she said, 'Dr. Bhatia, will you please speak to the gathering for two or three minutes?' I fell silent for a moment, then replied, 'All I can do in two or three minutes is stand up, say 'Sai Ram' and sit down.' 'Well,' she said, 'we do have our own discipline.' 'Yes,' I said, 'and I would not like to transgress that discipline, but I would like enough time to say something worthwhile.' Then, as if taking a great risk, she said, 'All right, you can talk for ten minutes.' It generally takes me that long to warm up. I replied, 'I have some beautiful stories of Swami's great love and would like to share them with you if you are interested.' So I stood up and began to talk. Looking at my watch, I saw that twenty minutes had passed. 'My time is up,' I said. 'No, no! Dr. Bhatia,' the audience called, 'please go on. We want to know more about Sai Baba's love.' So

I went on and on. Each time I tried to stop, they pressed me to continue. After I had talked for two hours, I saw the time was getting late. I said, 'Now I must stop.' 'No, no, go on,' they begged. But I said, 'No, we have our work tomorrow and we must stop.'

As we were leaving, Mrs. Biggart took my hand, 'I would like to show you something.' She led me through a door and we stood on a balcony with Miami beach spreading below, the ocean out in front. 'From here,' she told me, 'you can enjoy both beautiful sunrises and sunsets.' Suddenly a memory flooded back and my legs felt so weak I could scarcely stand. For years, Swami had been giving me a vision of a beautiful place such as this where, looking across the ocean to the east and to the west, I had enjoyed magnificent sunrises and sunsets. Now suddenly the vision had become a reality. What did it mean? Was something unbelievably wonderful going to happen to me?

"My heart overflowing with love for the brothers and sisters I left in America, I returned to Prashanti Nilayam on November 20, just before Swami's birthday -- November 23, 1993. I looked forward to the heavenly experience of sharing the joys of my month in America with my ever-loving Lord. This, I thought, was the supreme experience awaiting me. But, to my utter dismay, I found that the ever-loving Lord was not speaking to me. He would not even look at me. His eyes went over and behind me, but he didn't even see me. What could I do except keep quiet and wonder what I had done? How had I displeased him? Surely he would speak to me soon. Days passed -- a week, two weeks, three weeks. Still, he ignored my existence. I cried inwardly. 'Swami, Swami, my Lord. I cannot live without your loving recognition of my existence. Without your love, there is no charm left in life. I would rather die than be without you this way.' That was my prayer to him and I really began to think that if Swami didn't speak to me, I would end my life.

"A silent month and three days went by after my return. On December 23, just before Christmas, Swami took a family into the interview room, just one family -- an old couple, their son and daughter and their families. After a while, Swami opened the door, looked along the lines of men on the veranda and called one word, 'Bhatia.' Startled, I replied in a choked voice, 'Swami.' 'Bhatia.' 'Swami.' 'Come.' I stood up, stumbling, and rushed toward the door. Inside, Swami said, 'Sit down. I will show you everything.'

The old couple was celebrating their golden anniversary, so I sat and watched Swami producing *mangala sutras*, rings and other things, blessing the family in every way. Finally, Swami took the whole family inside the private room. I waited alone. Eventually they came out, the family sat down and Swami took me inside.

At last I was in the personal interview room with Swami. He sat on his chair and I sat on the floor in front of him. He looked into my eyes and asked me a question, 'Why do you feel that I don't love you?' I sat quietly before him, my hands folded. He repeated the question. 'Why do you feel that I don't love you? In your mind: this, that. Swami doesn't talk to me; Swami doesn't love me. You are my son. You are my child. I love you.' He took my head and put it in his lap and started patting and stroking it like a mother does a baby. As he did this, he said, 'No, Bhatia. Never feel that I don't love you. I love you, my child. You are my son. Remember, I am God, I am Love. Live in love. Live in love and you will live in God.' Looking at him, I said, 'Yes, Swami, I will live only in your love. There is nothing else in my life.'

"Then he said to me, 'What do you want?' I replied, 'Swami, I want nothing.' But he repeated, 'What do you want?' 'Swami, I want only you. You have given me everything. There is nothing else I want.' But he would not accept this answer and kept repeating his question. Eventually I said, 'Swami, do you promise to give me anything I want?' He said, 'Yes, now I will give you anything.' 'Well,' I said, 'I want to merge with you here and now. I do not want to leave this room, Swami. Please absorb me in you.' 'What?' he said, 'You have wife, you have daughters, you have your work. Do you want to desert your responsibilities? In the fullness of time, I will give you what you want. But it is selfish to want that now, shirking your responsibilities.' I saw that what he said was true. I was selfish in wanting liberation here and now. I withdrew my request and said, 'Swami, tell me why have you brought me into such a filthy world, so full of confusion and chaos? Please tell me that.' My master gave me another beautiful lesson when he said, 'I have brought you here to do my work.'

"So, this is what I tell my brothers and sisters who are working for Sai. He has brought us here into incarnation to do his work. How blessed we are. Each one of us has special work to do for his mission. We must find our Sai job and do it with all our hearts and with all the love we can give to it. And we must strictly and continuously follow the teachings of Swami.

"There I was, alone at Swami's feet, literally wetting his robe and his feet with my tears. He went on patting and patting me with love. When I could speak again, I said, 'I beg you, Swami, please give me the strength and the will and the love and the understanding to carry out my work as your instrument.' 'I will do it. I will do it,' he said. Then he put his hand under my collar and started stroking my spinal column with his fingers. I felt as if my *kundalini* were rising and rising. It seemed to go right up to the Crown Chakra and I felt that there was no space nor time. While massaging my back, he kept repeating, 'Bhatia, you are my son, I love you.' Then when he had me in this high, near-*samadhi* state, he rose to his feet and said, 'See what I am showing you.' I had let go my hold on his robe and was on my knees with folded hands looking at him. "While I watched, he vanished from my sight. He was simply not there any more. I could scarcely believe my eyes. He had vanished from where he stood; he had vanished from the room. I began to panic. What could I do? What will happen if I go out there alone and tell them that Swami has disappeared? They won't believe me. They will kill me. I felt very confused and afraid. Then, believe it or not, I saw Mother Parvati standing in front of me, just where Swami had stood. She was in a form I could not only see, but feel and touch with my hands. A beautiful woman with snowy white skin and an expression full of love, grace and compassion, she wore a greenish-yellow *sari* with golden embroidery. I fell at her lotus feet and kissed them. When I sat back on my knees, she put her hand on my head and spoke to me in the way that Swami had done. 'Don't worry, you are my son,' she said, 'I will take care of you. I love you. My child, I will always love you. Never worry.'"

Dr. Bhatia seemed almost carried away with the memory of the vision. I, too, felt transported to the feet of the beautiful Parvati, the goddess for whom I feel the greatest love. I could almost hear the sweet, loving tone of her divine voice. "How old did she look?" I asked Dr. Bhatia. He thought for a moment. "About thirty-two," he replied. He went on:

"Soon she disappeared and I saw Lord Siva standing in her place. He was about six feet, four inches tall with a huge, flowing black beard and dark hair that came down to his shoulders. He had the absolute face of a great yogi. While Parvati had been white, he was dark in color. I can only say that if she were the perfect 'she' of the universe, Siva was the perfect 'he.' They seemed made for each other. He was wearing a *dhoti*-like garment from his waist down; above the waist, he was bare. I fell at his feet and kissed the lower part of his legs. I continued for two or three minutes. He said nothing, but kept his hand on my head, just as Mother Parvati had done. I knew that he was giving me his divine blessing. I could feel the throb of the energy, love and grace flowing from him; I could hear the creative sound of the universe coming from inside him. *Aum*, aum, aum....

"Just when I felt I could take no more of his glorious, overpowering presence, I saw both of them standing before me -- Siva and Parvati, side by side. She put her hand on my head again and said, 'My child, we both love you. Don't worry, we will always take care of you.' Then they moved closer together and began to merge into one form. When they were completely one, *Siva-Shakti*, Swami himself emerged from them.

" 'You see,' he said, 'I am not just a man or a woman.' Then, thumping his chest, he said, 'I am God.' Then he pulled my head toward him and put it against his chest. I could hear the exact same sound of creation I had heard in Siva. It was as if the *Pranava Aum* sounded with every breath. He placed his hand on my head and I seemed to be transported to a place I did not know. There was no place, no time, no identity, no he, you, me or anything. There was only God, cool light and bliss. That was all he showed me that day.

"I started sobbing loudly and crying out, 'Swami, please, I can't take any more.' Lovingly, he looked at me and said, 'Hey, keep quiet! What will people think in the other room? They will think Swami is scolding Bhatia so much he is making him cry.' We were suddenly back to earth and he led me out of the doorway and past the curtain and into the other room. Standing there beside me, he called to one of the people there who had a camera, 'Take a photo of us.' Later he gave me the photograph. Was it a souvenir or a reminder? But how could I ever forget the greatest, most revealing experience of my life?"

When Dr. Naresh Bhatia finished, a complete silence reigned in the room. The story, the ringing tone of enthusiasm and joy in his voice, his genuine humility and love in the telling, had all transported us to the transcendental reality of being. Coming back to the mundane world was difficult.

My two Australian friends -- Neville Fredericks and Sheba Walker -- who were in the room and I had no doubts whatsoever of the truth of Bhatia's experience. Nor could anyone who had the privilege of hearing him doubt the genuine young disciple of Lord Sai -- Dr. Naresh Bhatia.

To watch again the golden robe
Move down the darshan line,
We are coming back to you, we say,
But how indeed can we come back
When we have never been away?

Your mansion is the Universe,
Your mansion is my heart,
You overflow the largest thing
You are the smallest part.
Where footprints on the sacred sands
Write alphabets of love,
We are flying back to you, we say,
But how, great Lord, can we fly back
When we have never been away?

You are the extra passenger in bus or car or train,
Your voice is in the winds that pass
And "Sai Ram" sings the rain.
To see once more the face of God
Brings meaning to the day,
We are turning back to you, we say,
But how in truth can we turn back
When we've never been away?

16

HEALTH, HARMONY AND HEALING

Serving each of us during our lives on earth are three main instruments, sometimes called the bodies, sheaths or *kosas*. The three are the physical body, the astral or emotional body and the mental body. Health of the physical body means harmony in the workings of all its various parts; similarly, health in the other two bodies requires the harmonious functioning of all their parts. But the three bodies, or instruments of the soul, are closely interlocked, linked or enmeshed together so that disharmony in one will cause disharmony in the others. If dis-ease is felt in the physical instrument, the basic cause may lie in some disharmony within the emotional body or the mental body. Likewise, the type of trouble -- dis-ease -- within either the emotional or mental bodies may be traced in its roots to disharmony in one of the other two instruments. When the individual enjoys perfect, radiant health, it means that the three instruments are each functioning in tune and all divinely knit together. They are a three-instrument orchestra functioning in perfect harmony.

Who controls the little orchestra that is so frequently getting out of tune and out of harmony? The one it serves. The one known as "the soul" to the English and as the *Atman* to the Hindus and the Theosophists. We regard the master of the orchestra as the true, real Self. In the teachings of the Avatar Sai Baba, this is the God within. It is fair to ask why this divine soul, awakening within us to the full consciousness of his Godhead, cannot control the instruments that are serving him? Why can't the real Self of the individual ensure that the instruments he is using in the earth-life are kept in good tune and good harmony? That is a good question, not easily answered.

Let us look at some cases of actual healing, or re-harmonizing, to see what we can understand about them.

Dorothy's Knees

"Unless you have both knees replaced," said the orthopaedic surgeon, "You will soon be in a wheelchair for the rest of your life." This very unpleasant prospect was even worse than the crutches Dorothy O'Brien had been using for a few years. The doctor explained that with the new plastic knees he would give her, she would be able to walk without the crutches. But they won't last forever, he explained. After a few years they will wear out and need to be replaced. Dorothy, not yet seventy, did not like the prospect of surgery and more operations in the years ahead. But life in a wheelchair was even less inviting. Is there no other answer, either in orthodox or alternative medicine? she wondered. For ten years she had tried every known cure for the crippling arthritis in her knee-joints. She asked the doctor, a kindly, compassionate man, "Is surgery the only possible way I can walk again?" He replied, "Short of divine intervention, there is no other way."

The words, "divine intervention," lit a tiny light of hope in her mind. A decade earlier, she, twin sister Moyia, and their beloved mother, Ruth O'Brien, had paid a visit to the ashram of Sathya Sai Baba in India. When they came into his presence, all three of them had immediately recognized in Sai Baba a divine man of power. Throughout the intervening years, Moyia had made yearly visits to Sai Baba. Mother Ruth was too old to make the journey; Dorothy was in charge of the "Sunshine Welfare and Rehabilitation Association" (SWARA) of Brisbane, and was unable to get away for more than one more visit. Moyia gave all her time to helping Dorothy in the occupational therapy work of SWARA. Yet both agreed she should take time off once a year to sit at the divine feet of their spiritual master in India. Swami always seemed delighted to see her and spoke lovingly of twin sister Dorothy and their saintly mother. The twin sisters were so devoted to their work of helping the handicapped, that neither had ever married. Living a selfless life of service, they seemed without fault. Without the knowledge and acceptance of karma, its action stretching through more than one lifetime, one might wonder why sweet, pure Dorothy would suffer such a crippling disease. A longtime friend of the twins, Valmai Worthington, who also helped at SWARA, was at the ashram in India at the time Dorothy heard the medical verdict about her knees. A woman of action, Valmai learned that Dorothy was in great pain and that friends were urging her to have the operation. Aware that Dorothy longed for divine help from Swami, Valmai asked him for help on her friend's behalf.

At a group interview, just after Swami had asked her about the twins, whom he called her "sisters," Valmai said boldly, "May I talk to you about Dorothy's knees, Swami?" Swami encouraged her to continue, so Valmai went on, "She is suffering a great pain and walking has become very difficult. A surgeon has recommended an operation. Should she have it, Swami?" "No, " Swami replied firmly, "No operation."

Immediately after the interview, Valmai phoned Brisbane to tell the twins the news. They received it with joy because his firm answer gave strong hope that the Lord himself would help Dorothy. Back at Prashanti Nilayam, Valmai wanted to make quite certain that she had understood Swami's words and his intention correctly. To ask him again would seem like checking him out. She hesitated until, a few days later, in the interview room again, she took courage and said, "Swami, I want to make sure I understood you correctly about Dorothy's knees. The surgeon says she must have an operation. Please tell me again what you said about that." Swami replied quite decisively, "No. No operation. I will operate. I will cure her."

Hearing about this second reply, Dorothy felt no doubt whatever about Swami's intention to cure her. She felt overjoyed and immediately phoned to cancel plans for the scheduled operation. The surgeon, an exceptionally understanding man, said he was happy for her but would be available should she need his help in future.

It seemed providential that one of their most trustworthy part-time helpers, Elma, could arrange to serve as manager of SWARA while Dorothy and Moyia were in India. Full of joy and faith, the twins and their spiritual sister, Valmai, arrived at Prashanti Nilayam in September, 1992.

My wife, Iris, and I were in residence at the ashram when they arrived late in the afternoon at their unit next door to ours in Roundhouse Five. At afternoon *darshan*, as Swami passed their line, he remarked to Valmai in a bright tone, "Ah, you've arrived and you have brought the twins with you." This sounded like a welcome and they all felt full of hope for an early interview.

It came a few days later. Dorothy was taken in a wheelchair to the door of the interview room and waited there among the other people who had been called. When Swami came back from darshan, he opened the door and called them all into the interview room. Valmai pushed Dorothy's wheelchair close to Swami's chair. Afterwards, she felt very guilty about doing this, but when Swami had seated everybody comfortably and materialized *vibhuti* for the women, he sat in his chair, happily smiling at the faces before him. Dorothy relates that he looked at her with great compassion and made several remarks about the bad condition of her knees. But he said comfortingly, "I will help, I will help."

After he had spoken to a few other people in the room, he stood up and went through the curtain to the private interview room, telling the twins and Valmai to follow him. Again, Valmai pushed the wheelchair through the doorway, bringing it close to Swami's feet as he sat in his own chair. A few other people were also called into the room and sat expectantly on chairs or on the floor, silently waiting to see what would happen. Swami stood up. Placing his hands firmly on Dorothy's knees -- one hand on each knee with palms downward -- he began to make circular motions, his hands still in contact with the knees. After a while, he raised his hands and continued the circular motion a few inches above each knee. This continued for some time while, presumably, the divine healing power of the Avatar passed from his hands into her knees. Then he dropped his hands to his sides and asked Dorothy in a gentle, compassionate voice, "Can you stand up?" The reply came from her lips, "I think I could with your help, Swami." He pushed her chair back a little to make room for her to stand; then he took her hands in his to help her rise. Feeling that the pain had gone from her knees, Dorothy stood up confidently on the floor. His next question was, "Can you walk now?" Her reply was, "I think I could with your help, Baba." "Come on then," he said, taking her arm lightly. Without pain and with complete confidence, she walked with the Lord across the room, through the doorway, up the step and across the floor to the people who were waiting in the outer interview room. Swinging open the main door, Swami led her out onto the veranda. There she stood for a few moments with Swami at her side and all eyes of the great crowd were upon her. She felt very elated. It was years since she had walked freely, without crutches, and after a few moments, Swami said to her, "Can you walk alone now?" "By your grace and through your power, I can."

And she walked -- through the great lines of people who were waiting for *bhajans* to begin. When the singing ended, Dorothy walked slowly all the way back to Roundhouse Five, where her unit was situated on the first floor. It was a triumphant walk. All the way people tried to touch her and talk to her; some with movie cameras recorded the first long march of the healed cripple.

Iris and I waited for her on the landing of the first floor of the Roundhouse. We watched her climb up the stairs towards us, holding the bannister with one hand but needing no other help. Her sweet face was alight with joy as she approached. We thought she would turn left into her own unit but instead she turned right and came into our room. Moyia, Valmai and others who were following, came in too. Some with cameras came and there was much celebration and rejoicing. In my own heart -- and

I suspect in Dorothy's and others' -- there was a flood of thanksgiving to the Lord for his divine healing that morning.

I have witnessed other cases where Swami has made cripples walk, but I did not find out what happened to them afterwards. But since the O'Brien twins are among our closest friends, I can bear witness that the lovely Dorothy O'Brien is still walking without the aid of wheelchair or crutches three years after her healing.

Susan and Little David

A young doctor I know, a Sai Baba devotee, told me he believes all genuine healing comes from God, that healing of body or mind is basically spiritual healing. Medical doctors and alternative healers may think they have cured a disease, but they have only played some part -- usually a small part -- to facilitate the flow of divine healing. Since God has the true welfare of the suffering one at heart, there can be no physical healing unless karma permits, for karma itself brings eventual healing, involving as it does a restoration of balance and harmony. If healing through karma is needed, the continuation of physical suffering may be the truest healing. We also need to understand that the one God works in various forms -- as the Godman Jesus, as the Godman Sai Baba and so on. He may work through the God within the patient or through the more evolved divine center in a healer. In fact, the return to harmony, ease and good health may come through more than one channel. Furthermore, there may be terrible suffering in more than one person before the page of karma is turned and full healing comes to remove suffering.

This was the case with Sue and little David. At the time their sufferings began, Sue Cotis, husband Barry and two small children -- a seven year old daughter and five year old son, David -- lived on the Gold Coast, a beautiful part of Queensland where thirty miles of golden beaches are caressed by the Pacific Ocean. Sue was living happily and peacefully, with no idea that the gods, not of Olympus but of Karma, were about to strike a devastating blow.

Toward the end of 1988, when David was five and a half, he received the immunization injections given to most children his age -- four altogether. Just two days before the shots, he had gotten two amalgam dental fillings. Susan thinks they may have touched off the terrible nerve disorders that followed though no medical authority has told her so. A few days later, David began to have mild, daily seizures that affected his head, eyes and arms. After a battery of tests, no clue to the trouble could be found. Thinking it could be the beginning of epilepsy, doctors prescribed the standard drugs. But instead of improving, the seizures worsened. Frequently, David fell flat on his back. When medical specialists could not help, Sue and Barry tried every alternative medical treatment available. The range in Brisbane was not very great. They tried homeopathy, acupuncture, Chinese herbs. They consulted dieticians and neuro-surgeons. But something worse than ordinary epilepsy seemed to have seized the boy. David became more vacant, more agitated and angry and his falling fits increased in number and intensity.

Since caring for him was a full time job, Sue had to give up the job she had taken to help the family budget. To take up the slack, Barry worked longer hours as an insurance counsellor, leaving the major portion of David's care to Sue. David was violent. He attacked his mother and sister Maria; he broke his own toys and hers. Maria, only seven, didn't understand what was happening and began hitting her brother. She blamed her parents for the change, saying, "What have you done with my little brother?" -- as if he had gone away and a demon had taken his place.

Sue continued to go to any healer recommended by a friend; some were a great distance away. This could be trying because the boy was now hyperactive and had lost control of both bladder and bowels. Like the medical doctors, the healers shook their heads and proclaimed the boy incurable. But Sue would not give up hope. Sometimes she heard friends say she was too attached to David, that she encouraged him to exaggerate his symptoms to gain her attention. Others said she should accept the verdict that he was incurable.

A light shone in the darkness when a clairvoyant told her David would eventually get well, but he would get worse before he got better. He got worse and conditions at home became a nightmare. Sue tried treatments with an official government psychologist, a Christian counsellor, a holistic healing center. Nothing helped. The desperate attempts to find a cure cost a great deal and although Barry worked long hours, their money was running low. So was Susan's energy. She was near the breaking point.

In February, 1990, fifteen months after his trouble began, David stopped talking altogether. His speech had been deteriorating; at age six and a half, he was completely dumb and all other symptoms of his mysterious, undiagnosable complaint had grown worse and worse. How much longer can we bear it and remain sane? Sue wondered. She had been a member of the Uniting Church but found no help in religion.

At this time, Sue first heard about Sai Baba. A former yoga teacher advised her to take David straight to India to Sai Baba's ashram. He said with great confidence, "If Karma allows, Baba will certainly cure your David." He told her to seek out the Sai Baba Center in Brisbane, read all the books she could about the divine teacher and healer and pray for Sai Baba's help. He also wrote details for getting to the ashram and told her the approximate cost. She and Barry had no money left to buy tickets to India, and even if the money had miraculously appeared, Sue knew she didn't have the strength to handle the little boy alone on a long air trip to India.

But she did find the Sai Baba Center in Brisbane and met the positive helper, Valmai Worthington. Valmai loaned Sue all her Sai Baba books and told her she must write a letter to Sai Baba every day and pray daily to him from the depths of her heart. Moreover, twice a day without fail, she must give the boy half a teaspoon of vibhuti (Swami's sacred ash) in water. "Have faith," she said. "Swami has cured incurable diseases by absent healing." Valmai inspired Sue by her confident tone.

From that day, Sue studied the Sai Baba books and gave young David the prescribed daily treatment. She prayed with all her heart to Swami and wrote him letters daily asking for help.

For some reason, Susan's hopes began to soar and she felt inwardly that positive things were about to happen. But she felt upset when her husband gave the story of David to a newspaper reporter and it appeared in a leading Brisbane daily. Yet, though she hated the publicity, it did bring one very positive result, making her think perhaps Barry had been inspired by Sai Baba. Susan received a letter from a woman who had read the article, saying she was a Christian healer and would be happy to treat David for free. Grateful, Susan began taking her son for treatment twice a week. The healer gave him massages and used color therapy; she also suggested games the mother could play with David each evening; she recommended music to accompany the games.

The cure was not immediate. The seizures continued daily but seemed to grow less intense. Religiously, Sue followed the recommended Sai therapy of daily prayer, letter writing to the Lord and twice-daily doses of vibhuti.

Then the great day dawned. November, 1990. The healer, who had become a good friend, said to Sue one morning "I'll take David to the beach today and play with him while you do your shopping." Sue jumped at the chance. No one had ever offered to care for the boy to give her a break. In the afternoon, the healer returned with David. She said, "Sue, you may think I'm silly, but I took David into the sea and gave him a Christian baptism. I washed him all over with sea water, saying as I did so the words of the baptism sacrament." Susan was very pleased to hear this, because with all their trouble, they had never found time to baptize David. "From that very day," Sue remembers, "David's seizures, which had occurred regularly night and morning, ceased." At first Susan and Barry could scarcely believe that their son's horrendous nightmare and their own agonies had come to an end. But as the days and weeks passed with no more signs of the symptoms, they knew God had given them a great healing miracle. Their hearts were full of gladness and gratitude.

When Sue finished telling me her story, I asked if she gave credit for the healing to Sai Baba or to Jesus. She answered, "To both. I thank both from the bottom of my heart." Then, with a flash of insight, she added, "Surely they are both the same." "Yes, you are right," I replied, "Swami teaches us that we are all one and, therefore, the Godmen are one at whatever period of time they came to earth. It follows that you can be a true Christian and a Sai devotee at the same time."

David's devastating ordeal and its happy conclusion made Susan a devotee of Sai Baba -- and, undoubtedly, a more understanding and truer Christian. She demonstrated this by doing volunteer work with the O'Brien twins and Valmai Worthington at SWARA.

One thing we must clearly understand is that there is no jealousy or rivalry between the *Avataric* manifestations of God.

Healing Mysteries

I sometimes wonder what we really know about the mysteries of healing -- its process, the depth and scope of its meaning. In 1990, Isaac was practicing medicine in Sydney, Australia, when what he calls "the incident" took place. His parents lived in Melbourne where, though born in Eastern Europe, Isaac had graduated from the University of Melbourne.

The incident began when his mother, a sixty-five year old research industrial chemist, was leaving a crowded concert. Moving along the aisle, she tripped over an umbrella or walking stick. She fell heavily to the floor and broke her hip. The nasty accident was a climax of three misfortunes. She had fallen and broken her wrist a few weeks earlier; shortly afterwards, the

Melbourne home of her and her husband had been burgled and a number of precious personal things taken; next came her fall in the concert hall.

She was a frail, delicate woman. Doctors found that the neck of the femur bone of her thigh was badly broken near the hip. Dr. Isaac says, however, that she was fortunate in that a very good surgeon was on duty to perform the operation on the broken bone. Isaac's father called from Melbourne to tell him about the accident, assuring him that his mother was in the care of a competent surgeon in a very good hospital. Isaac phoned the hospital and spoke with his mother just after she came out of the anaesthetic. Under the circumstances, she seemed okay and Isaac didn't worry. He phoned again the next day to check on her progress. First he contacted the sisters' station and was alarmed to hear that three complications had arisen. Her diabetes was out of control; her blood pressure was high; and she had developed pneumonia. Isaac asked to speak to his mother. She sounded very weak and distant. His former medical experience and his own intuition told him that his mother was going to die. This devastating thought numbed his mind. He tried to think but thoughts would not come. All he could do was to feel with certainty that he did not want to lose his mother. Many things had to be settled between them, as he put it. He could not lose her. Suddenly, a thought came to him. He found the phone number of a friend in Melbourne -- a clairvoyant who was also a healer. In the past, he had learned to respect her insights into the inner side of illness and healing. He phoned her, hoping she would give him some instructions that would help him save his mother's life.

Indeed, she did just that. Dr. Isaac says, "She told me to go into a meditative state and to have a mental monologue with my mother. I was to attempt to resolve our conflicts of the past, forgiving her for things I saw as wrongs to me. Through it all, I was to send her a great deal of love. That wasn't difficult because I had a great deal of love for my mother. I concentrated on sending her streams of it. She also told me to contact the disease entity and to talk directly to it. I was very determined to heal my mother. I was not prepared to lose her because I felt there was a lot of unfinished business between us. Things had not always been easy between my mother and me, but now I attempted to put that aside -- to wash it out and forgive her entirely. I conversed with the disease entity in a very forthright manner. Using all my strength and will, I confronted it and directed it to leave my mother alone. When I went into this meditation, I was quite prepared to take all the time required -- all night if necessary. But after forty minutes, I knew the job was done. I had somehow managed to beat the disease entity, convincing it to leave my mother. Although I could have continued with this inner activity into which I had put my heart, mind and willpower, I felt that the task was accomplished. The entity had withdrawn, I thought, and anything further I did would be superfluous. I finished at about eleven o'clock and went to bed.

"The following afternoon I phoned my mother to see how she was. The sound of her voice told me she was healed. She sounded positive, full of energy and vitality. After talking for a while, she told me of an experience she had just had. While she was lying in her hospital bed, she had experienced a blue light that seemed to emanate from a diamond-shaped spot in her forehead between her eyes. It was not with her physical eyes that she saw this spot, but with a spiritual vision. The light filled her body and with it came bliss -- a kind of bliss she had never experienced before. She felt overjoyed with the experience but asked me not to tell my father because he would probably think she was having an hallucination." She was at a loss to understand the experience because she had not been practicing any religion. Her only religious activity had been the ritualistic one of keeping the Jewish festivities, which was more social than spiritual. Like her husband, her training and education had been scientific and they were agnostics.

Dr. Isaac says when he phoned his mother the next day, she was delighted the experience of light from the blue diamond in her forehead had been repeated. Although not as intense as the first time, it was otherwise exactly the same experience. Now instead of being low, depressed and sinking towards her death, she was quite jovial and happy. From that day, she went forward slowly but surely and made a good recovery.

With his orthodox training as a medical doctor, Isaac might well have scoffed at the idea of talking to a disease entity, but he was open-minded enough to follow the psychic's advice. He feels quite sure it was through this that his mother returned to good health. Otherwise she would have died, Isaac feels sure.

Theosophists would probably say that he spoke to the physical elemental, which is like the factory manager of the physical body. Medicine men of the Australian aborigines might say that he spoke to the organs of the physical body themselves, in the same way they talk or sing a broken bone in the physical body to go back into place and heal itself (* Footnote. See Chapter 13 in the book, *Mutant Message Down Under*, by Marlowe Morgan.) But there are leading spiritual teachers, including Sai Baba of Shirdi, who speak of the reality of disease entities. Unlike his parents, Isaac is deeply interested in the spiritual dimension of the macrocosm and the microcosm. On his way to Avatar Sathya Sai Baba, he spent time absorbing the teachings of Paramahansa Yogananda and Paramahansa Ramakrishna. Now he is a fully committed devotee of Sathya Sai Baba.

I agree with my young doctor friend that all true healing comes from God, but God is not necessarily out there somewhere away from us. He is inside us and is, in fact, our true Selves. So, in brief, we heal ourselves. But techniques seem to be needed. The technique I know and have proved by personal experience to keep body and mind healthy, is something I have learned from various types of yoga. Briefly it is this. There is a cosmic energy available for our use. In *Sanskrit,* it is called *prana* and goes by that name in all the *yogas*. This energy, this prana, goes wherever the mind directs it. Consciousness is the vehicle on which it travels; intention, plus willpower from our divine inner selves, is the engine that drives the vehicle. To keep the body and mind healthy -- to overcome or prevent blockages in the flow of energies through our physical, etheric and mental vehicles -- send prana to every part of the body. It goes wherever our consciousness takes it. To keep healthy, we must do this every day. If we feel a malady in some part of the body, which means there is a block of energy there, we direct the prana there in greater measure. This is the secret of the great yogis. If we fail to carry out this therapy effectively, we must seek outside healing help. While unrealized souls -- or what I call the lesser gods with amnesia -- may give some assistance, the only true healing comes from God. And the best source of that divine help is the Avatar Sai Baba. While many know of his work as the great healer, some may ask why he'd heal many diseases, even incurable ones, and yet fails to heal others. Is it possible that an Avatar can fail in what he sets out to do? There are times when he assures the relatives of a sick person that he is taking care of the patient and if somebody asks him directly, "Will you heal the patient, Swami?" He may reply, "Yes. Yes, I will heal him." Yet sometimes, despite this clear statement, the patient dies. How can we understand and accept such a thing, while still believing the Avatar cannot fail?

Surely to heal can mean only one thing: To bring the disease or disharmony back to harmony to allow the person to function on earth in a normal way. But is there another meaning? I found that indeed there was when I recently read an English translation of Plato's work, "The Last Days of Socrates." The clue is found in the final few pages. Socrates is drinking the hemlock, as condemned to do by the Greek government in Athens. Gathered in the room where he is drinking the poison are some of his many close friends. One of them is Crito. While the hemlock poison creeps slowly up Socrates' body, beginning with his feet, the great master is trying to educate those around him on the deeper meanings of life and death. Crito asks him what he wants done with him after his death. Socrates replies, "Whatever you like, if you can catch me." Then he remarks that Crito will not understand that Socrates is not his body. Only his body will die and he does not mind what they do with that. Just before the deadly hemlock reaches the vital areas and takes the life of the great philosopher, he says something that, for me, clarifies the problem before us. Cold was spreading as far as his waist when Socrates uncovered his face, for he had previously covered it up. Now he said his last words, "Crito, we ought to offer a cock to Aesclepius. See to it and don't forget." "It shall be done," said Crito. "Are you sure there is nothing else?" Socrates made no reply to this question. He had covered his face again. After a little while, Crito rose and uncovered it. He saw that the eyes were fixed. Seeing this, he closed Socrates' mouth and eyes. "Such was the end of our comrade," says the writer, "Who was, we may fairly say, of all those whom we knew in our time, the bravest and also the wisest and most upright man." There is a footnote which explains that Aesclepius was the god of healing for the ancient Greeks. The sacrifice of a cock, or a rooster, which Socrates requests at the moment of his death, was a thanks offering to the god of healing because Socrates regarded death as the healing of the disease of life. I have no doubt the merciful Sathya Sai Baba looks at it in this way when he equates the death of some person with the healing.

17

BANGAROO

My very dear Iris,

I have had plenty of evidence from friends more sensitive to other worlds than I am, that you visit our old home here in Hazelbrook and other places whenever you have a good purpose for doing so. So I wonder if you are here now, reading this letter as I struggle to write it. I say 'struggle' because the letter is for publication. I want to avoid repeating things already told in earlier books. My aim is to spotlight aspects of our great journey together, in which you played a significant part. I want to project a truer picture of you than I have done in my previous writings. So I want to share with you, in memory, a few untold aspects of events that we enjoyed together during our happy wanderings. I shall imagine that you are sitting here by me, as indeed you well may be.

You will remember, no doubt, that Swami told us in the early days that in our last lives we had been Indian boys and very close friends. He said at another time we had lived in the same community as the parents of Shirdi Sai Baba. Because you once saved my life in our days as young Indians, I had vowed, Swami said, to seek you out in our next life and give you all the help I could. But I wonder now who helped whom? It seems in retrospect, don't you think, to have been a mutual helping -- giving and receiving, teaching and learning.

Our Lord made the point that we had almost met each other on a number of occasions before the actual meeting took place. We discussed that, remember? We thought about the times our paths crossed in northern England early in the days of World War II; later on, how remarkable it was that we were students of the same Yoga School in Sydney for two or three years before we actually met in January, 1958 -- because both of us made the same error about the day of the school's resumption after the Christmas break. Nobody except you or I made that mistake. I wonder now if the event was engineered by Swami. He often makes the point that all important events in this life have to take place at the right time. Time is a very important factor. I know that it was so on this occasion because I would not have been ready for the great event any earlier. We were meant, you and I, to be close companions in the vital chapters of the spiritual search that led to the discovery of our shining star, our *sadguru* Sai Baba.

You will recall how we searched for a church that would give a spiritual dimension to our marriage. We thought it was rather a hopeless task but, no doubt by the grace of God, we eventually found one in the Liberal Catholic Church. Though, in 1959, we had what my mother would call a marriage made in heaven, I think finding and becoming members of the Liberal Catholic Church was important, becoming part of the divine design that governs our lives, or, as Shakespeare says, "That divinity that shapes our ends, rough hew them as we will." Through becoming members and friends of the priesthood of that church, we eventually became members of the Australian branch of the Theosophical Society and that, as you know well, was a link in the chain that lead to Adyar, India and Sathya Sai Baba.

I have described our journey across half the world to find him -- our star of meaning -- in earlier books. So I will not repeat those things here. Instead, I will jump into the journey during our first winter in the south of Spain. Remember the Moorish house that opened onto the beach at the Costa del Sol? Even though rent was cheap in the little village of Rincon and groceries were inexpensive in beautiful Malaga, ten miles away, petrol was expensive except in Gibraltar, which was too far to visit often. We had to watch our pennies.

I sat writing happily in the room that overlooked the sea, but we both knew my work would bring in no money until we visited England the next spring. So it would be wise for us to earn something in Spain. But how could we in the sleepy, remote little village? You thought of teaching *hatha yoga*, which you were fully qualified to do. But Generalissimo Franco was still firmly in the Spanish saddle, which meant that the church was powerful and narrow. Yoga was regarded as the work of the devil -- and, therefore, taboo. Advertising classes in Malaga would not be safe. Fortunately, however, wintering in the village were a good many people from elsewhere -- Canada, England, Switzerland and America. They all seemed keen to learn yoga. Perhaps the keenest of all was Sandy, a psychoanalyst from New York.

Soon your classes were established and flourishing in one of the rooms of our house. Raphael, a young Spaniard from Malaga, heard about them and rode his motorscooter along the winding coast road from Malaga, never missing a class. He became your most steady pupil and our close friend. Two priests who lived in a house on the edge of the village heard about the strange thing happening at our place. They came in black robes reaching to their boots to see what yoga was all about. But our next door neighbor, a young American woman, Dot, intercepted them, warning them that if they looked in, they would see much bare female flesh. This was true because one of the pupils, a Swiss woman, did yoga in her bikini. At any rate, the priests decided that discretion was the better part of valor so, with disappointment registered on their faces, they beat a retreat to their house on the hill.

No doubt you recall how Raphael arrived one day with a very frightened young man on his pillion. Since we knew yoga, Raphael hoped we would be able to help him. The man had begun to wake in the middle of the night to find himself floating up near the ceiling, looking down at his body on the bed. Very frightened, he went to his priest who said it was the work of the devil and all he could do was pray. We assured the young man that many people travel out of their bodies in this way -- and that many more wish they could. We told him that the experience, known generally as out-of-the-body experience (O.B.E. for short) was the subject of study by the highly respectable Society for Psychical Research in London, particularly by the Society's

Oxford branch. (Later, we visited the branch, conducted by young Oxford graduates, and I wrote an article about this for a women's journal in Fleet Street.) We reassured the frightened young Spaniard that the devil had nothing to do with his OBEs and that he was a lucky man to have the gift. His haunted expression changed to smiles and he went happily back to his home in Malaga.

It was an unexpected bonus for the yoga classes to bring help to this distressed young man, in addition to fulfilling its purpose of helping us through a tight economic period.

Another time, you helped our journey in a practical way in England, during the spring of 1961. We arrived in Coomb Springs at Kingston-on-Thames, a few miles from London. You took a short course in catering so that you could become the catering officer for the Subud community there. Apart from helping us financially, that had a long term effect -- a very important one. When later we went to the Theosophical Society headquarters at Adyar, near Madras in India, it assured you of the job of superintendent of Leadbeater Chambers, which, again, was a boon to the financial side of our venture.

But that job had one side for which you had no previous experience: the handling of the big staff of local servants employed at Leadbeater Chambers. Some were honest and reliable, but others were full of guile and adept in the art of purloining and hiding small articles, such as jewelry, which they took from the bedrooms of people who came from western countries to stay at the Chambers. You had, perforce, to be a detective as well as a controller, caterer and superintendent.

Despite all that, you managed to attend the lectures at the School of the Wisdom. When the director of studies, Dr. I. K. Taimni excused you from doing the research paper that was part of the School curriculum, you did it anyway, choosing the subject of Divine Love. I remember how delighted Dr Taimni was when you read that paper aloud, with its quotations from many different spiritual masters through the centuries.

I remember something I first realized after Swami opened me to the reality and experience of Divine Love: the way our director's face used to shine whenever he spoke of this subject and how he tried once to teach us Narada's *Bhakti Sutras,* dealing with the yoga path of love and devotion. But, being somewhat stuck on the expansion of consciousness, none of the students, including myself, showed much interest. I feel the good doctor of science, a learned occultist himself, must have at some time been with a great teacher who opened his heart to divine love.

It certainly was a happy, uplifting, elevating time -- those six months of imbibing ancient wisdom at the School and hearing the fine lectures given by the delegates to the big international convention during that Christmas time.

Later, after we made our tour of the Indian ashrams and came to Sai Baba, things had to change. We wanted to spend as much time as possible with him, both at his ashram and travelling, so it became necessary for you to give up your job at Leadbeater Chambers.

Then came our time at the beautiful Olcott Bungalow in a remote corner of the 250-acre Theosophical estate overlooking the sea. Both our jobs then were in interesting and enlightening research. I had been given a Writer's Fellowship to do biographies on each of the founders of the Society, Madame H. B. Blavatsky and Colonel H. S. Olcott. I was also to write radio talks for America on aspects of Theosophy. In the study of books from the great library and documents from the archives, we learned a great deal about the Theosophical Society -- its origins, purpose, meaning and the work it did in the early days. We learned, too, about the part the great Masters of the White Lodge played in the foundation and sustenance of the Society in its early years. It seemed as if the founders were still living and as if the two Masters who played the greatest part in bringing the Society into existence might appear as they sometimes did to the early workers: tall, majestic Master Morya riding upon a horse; or, Master Kuthumi, suddenly materializing before them out of thin air. Astral travel and the materialization of astral bodies were second nature to them. Remember, you had some visions of Madame H. B Blavatsky in which she spoke to you. This was a bonus for the great help you gave me in the research for my writings. A bonus for both of us was an increased awareness of the depths of Theosophy, and the organization that brought it to the world. I think you'll agree that it gave us a good foundation for what was to follow: Swami's wonderful presentation and personal demonstration of the *Sanathana Dharma* or Ancient Wisdom.

Though the years we spent with the Avatar may not have brought the constant bliss you are enjoying now, they were full of happiness and did have their occasional highlights of joy. Do you remember a picnic, for instance, with Swami and a few others in the bright, sun-kissed wood when you prepared an orange for him, dividing it into segments so that he could easily take one? Then as he passed, you offered it to him. Often he rejects such offers, but this time he took one, with the words, "Thanks, Bangaroo." I was standing nearby and was as thrilled for you as you must have been for yourself. He had never used the term, "Bangaroo," meaning "golden one" to me, nor have I ever heard him use it to anybody else, though doubtless he has. It is always a supreme joy to have Swami near, speaking to you, but I think his calling you "golden one" must have thrilled you beyond measure.

Now that you are with him always, over there in the realms of gold, do you ever bother thinking about some of the little things that pleased or amused or puzzled us when we were his companions on earth? Does it ever cross your mind how, in the early days when we were travelling with him in his car, he taught you a Hindi song? Then, on our return journey from a conference in Bombay -- the first big Sai Conference -- you had the honor of sitting next to Swami in the giant-sized room of a royal palace. A large crowd sat at a meal and he alarmed you by asking you to sing the Hindi song he had taught you. You were too shy to do

it until he said he would help you. He started you off, then he left
you singing alone and people crowded in from other rooms to
hear Swami's western pupil singing a Hindi song. You got
through it with flying colors. It was then that someone asked
Swami who I was. He said, "He's a German Sanskrit pundit." I
never understood that, and still do not. But I know that no word
from him can be fruitless or meaningless.

Two years later, in the middle of 1970, we finally decided, with
grim determination, to take the step of leaving Swami and
returning home to Australia. We felt unable to break the Sai-link
immediately, so decided to travel by way of England and
America where we had friends of the Sai following. As we said
goodbye to him (he seemed to understand immediately and
completely our practical reasons for going), I felt it would be a
good thing for me to have a longer perspective on Sai Baba, India
and all that had happened to us there. We had changed, our lives
had changed, but in the cool, objective, down-to-earth world of
the west, would I find that I had been living in some kind of
hypnotic dream? Would I laugh at my idea, my conviction that
Sathya Sai Baba was God on earth? It would be a good test to
spend some time away from him in a very different setting. You,
however, seemed to see things in a very different way. All that
concerned you was how soon we could return to him. You even
asked him that. You had no doubt that we wanted to return. This
shows me that you had more faith and surrender than I had. Or
perhaps I should say, you had transcended the mind more than I
had. You had "beheaded yourself," as the great Kabir put it, more
thoroughly than I had.

Let's take a brief look at what happened on our return home to
Australia. I always thought we went there for your roots, rather
than mine. Though born in England, you had a greater love of the
Australian scene than I did. You even admired the aboriginal
culture, whereas I knew nothing about it. I wonder now if you
spent a former life among the Aborigines -- quite possible since
they have been here for forty or fifty thousand years. Further,

your mother and sister waited in Australia, while my immediate family had vanished. My parents and sisters had "crossed the Jordan," as General Montgomery used to term it, and my son Richard was at university abroad.

From an economic and financial standpoint, living in Australia was different from living in India. I had reached retirement age, sixty-five, when our home-bound plane touched down in Sydney. There was no point in looking for a job. Perhaps I could get freelance journalistic work with newspapers or magazines. But, for that, I would have to write about subjects that would bring a monetary return. I strongly desired to go on writing on spiritual subjects, which bring in little or no money. You wanted me to do that, too. So you solved the problem by getting a job as matron of a nursing home. Such positions supplied a flat for the matron and her family to live in, usually attached to the nursing home, or close by. The first location was in the beautiful Blue Mountains not far from Sydney. Even with your managerial and nursing skills, added to a little help from my advertising experience, it took two years to bring the nursing home to full capacity. By that time, we had had enough of what seemed, in your words, "the spiritual desert of Australia." We longed to be back with Swami, so you got a six-month leave of absence.

Off to India we flew, arriving just in time for one of Swami's delightful and elevating summer courses in spirituality and Indian culture.

Being with Swami brought meaning back into our lives. We overstayed the six months, telling the nursing home owners we would be away another three months. Just before we left for home -- at the end of nine months -- we were having a farewell talk with Swami. You remarked that you had to get back to work. Swami surprised us both by saying, "Yes, get work." Since you had a position to return to, we wondered what he meant. But he knew something, as usual, that we did not know.

A change in the political and economic situation in Australia had led the three owner-directors to sell the nursing home. But within a few weeks of our return you were matron of a bigger nursing home, with a larger apartment for us, in the western suburbs of Sydney.

The time in India had provided me with enough material for another book. With the living accommodation that came to us through your position, I was able to get on with the writing. During our period in the Blue Mountains, helped by a mortgage at a special low interest rate from my war service, we had been able to buy a delightful little house in the lower Blue Mountains. We let this to tenants and the rent supplemented our income, providing all we needed for the simple form of life we had adopted. You were doing so well at running the nursing home that during the next three years, the owner of the home sent us both on two tours of the United States to attend conferences and visit places of interest in America, Canada and Mexico.

Two special joys came out of this travel bonus from the nursing home owner. It enabled us to spend time with one whom Swami called "my twin soul," that is, my sister, Leone, and also with the late, saintly Hilda Charlton. We had met her on our first visit to Swami in Madras in 1965 and when we saw her again about twelve years later, she was conducting what must have been the largest Sai Baba center in the world. This she held in New York in the great cathedral of John the Divine.

I remember in the late seventies, we left that nursing home and made another visit to Swami for a long stay. At the same time I hoped to get on with a book I was writing. I remember that after we had been with him for some time and had moved into a beautiful little house he gave us in the Brindavan ashram, we were able to spend many hours of the day in his company. But I was not able to write the book I had planned to do. I have no doubt you remember the shock we both got when sitting in our house one day. I said to you, "I find it impossible to sit here at a typewriter when I could be in Swami's company. I think we will have to go to Madras, take a flat at the Theosophical

Headquarters, Adyar, where I can be near the library for reference. There I'll have many undisturbed hours to write in a tranquil atmosphere. We can come back to Swami after a few months." You looked rather sad at the thought of leaving him, but you agreed. In fact, we were both sad, but we felt it was something we had to do. Later that same day, Swami paid us a visit and almost the first thing he said was, "Yes, I agree that you must go to Adyar to get on with your book." In fact he continued the conversation we had had earlier as if he had been in it. We knew he could be anywhere and hear anything he wished, but it was a shock when he demonstrated his omnipresence so specifically and pointedly.

We went as planned and as he agreed. But a time came when, although the book was written, we regretted the months we had lost of our Lord's company. "But he is always with us," we told each other, yet we both knew that the physical presence of the Avatar is something special and rare.

We decided that on our return to Australia, you would retire from nursing home management and we would live in our little house in the middle of its spreading lawns and gardens in the lower Blue Mountains. But your fame had gone before you; an owner dug you out and begged you to take charge of two nursing homes, both situated in the midst of a big garden, in the northern suburbs of Sydney. You agreed to do it for one year on condition that we could return to the Blue Mountains for weekends.

The year passed pleasantly enough and then we settled down quietly in our mountain home. But Swami does not allow his devotees who have come to earth specially to work for him, to rest lazily on their laurels. Within a few months, we helped start a Sai Baba center at the home of an Indian doctor in the area. Then when that doctor left to take his family to live at the ashram and work for Swami, we helped another Indian doctor start a Sai center in his home. That center is still going.

As flowers spring up in the desert in spring, Sathya Sai centers were appearing in Sydney and its environs. We felt the Sai gardens would continue to spread and Australia could never be called a spiritual desert again.

It is worth sharing with readers of this letter how Swami, who is often an absent healer, can also be an absent real-estate agent. I will not remind you, my dear, of the painful reasons why we had to sell our little house and move further up the mountains. We were in India visiting Swami just after our decision to do this. He always seemed very close to us, like a good father and mother and dearest friend. So one day we dared to say to him, "Swami, will you help sell our house?" Looking a bit surprised, he said, "What? Now? The market in Sydney is flat, very flat. You should leave it for a year." Does he know the state of the retail market everywhere in the world? we wondered. We told him why we must sell it straightaway. So he said, "Right. How much do you want for it?" When we told him, he said, "All right, you'll get that. Don't sell it for less."

Soon after our return, we put the house on the market with a local agent. When he asked us the price we wanted, we told him. It was Swami's price. He seemed a bit surprised but was even more surprised when the very first person he brought to see the house, bought it -- without any haggling. It was Swami's price. After searching in the higher mountains, we found and purchased a house at Hazelbrook. Then, on our next visit to Swami, we thanked him for helping us find the house. "Yes," he replied, "It suits you well." Then he described the house and grounds just as if he were living in it with us, which, of course, we know he is doing, unseen.

At Hazelbrook, we started a new Sathya Sai center which grew so much that it eventually had to move to bigger premises at Lawson, the next town up the mountains, a ten-minute drive from Hazelbrook.

In the various Sathya Sai centers we started in the Blue Mountains, you and I, as a team, were expected to lead the study and discussion circles. After several years, we thought there should be a change, but people wouldn't give us a rest. I think it was because we were able to tell anecdotes about our time with Swami to illustrate the teachings we studied. This, they said, seemed to bring Swami close to them.

Another way I feel you did much worthwhile work for the Sai mission, was in telephone counselling. Through my books, my name was well-known. Since my telephone number could easily be located in the Blue Mountains directory, people with problems would frequently phone. You took the calls and took me from my writing only when there was something you could not handle yourself. This was rare, and you never seemed to grow tired of helping and counselling. If the people calling wanted very much to talk to me, you would tell them to come to the Sai Baba meeting held every week, promising that I would talk to them there. Thus, you saved me many interruptions in my writing. Besides helping many people, you brought numbers of them into membership at our Sathya Sai center.

Do you remember how, during our last visit to Swami together, he told us that he was now securely in our hearts and in our lives so that we didn't need to make the strenuous, troublesome, expensive journey to India to see him? You told me afterwards that even so, you must go sometime to see him again, to see his face and feel the happiness of his presence.

As it turned out in the divine design of our lives, the next journey you made to India did not involve the expense and trouble of air and car travel.

When you first became sick enough to be taken to the hospital, early in April, 1994, neither of us thought for a moment that it was sickness unto death. In fact, you had often said I would die before you, not only because I was older but because, you said, you could cope better alone than I could -- which was true. But man's plans and God's plans are usually different things. Even up to a week before you died, you were maintaining with strenuous determination and will power that you were not going to die. I supported you, believing I was assisting in your positive thinking and helping you to hold onto life. But in the end, I realized I was helping to hold you back in a life of pain and weakness.   I realized I must leave it to Swami's will and must not be selfish enough to hold you back simply because I could not visualize life without you. So it was my love and compassion for you that made me say one day, "I release you. I want you to stay, but whatever is God's will must be done. So I release you." You looked at me with gratitude in your eyes and simply replied, "Thank you."

I think it was the next evening, or perhaps the one following, I sat by your bed in the nursing home. Linda Walker, who seemed like our Sai daughter, had her arm around you, cradling you in a semi-sitting position and doing her best to nurture you. You said in a quiet voice, "I'm leaving now." And, as you left your body, there was a glimmer of golden light on the photo of Swami that hung on the wall above your head. I knew you had gone; the doctor confirmed it; but I stood looking at your body for a long time. It was now an empty shell, I knew, but it was the appearance through which I had known and loved you for thirty-six years.

The next day, I had a better and fuller description of your passing, Iris, from one who had not even been there. It came from Joan Moylan. She phoned me from somewhere in Queensland to say that Swami had sent a golden beam over the bed, covering Iris and the two of us who were present, glimmering on the picture above her bed. In that golden beam, Swami had stood and received Iris' soul as she left her physical body and came to him.

You shed your painful body on the evening of the 22nd August, 1994, and twenty-four hours later, on 23rd August, you appeared in the evening to your clairvoyant friend, Rhonda Gates, in her home in northern New South Wales. Your words, as she reported them to me later, were, "I've had a wonderful breakthrough. I'm in a state of great bliss, but poor Howard is devastated." Thank you for those words, assuring me that you were in a state of bliss. They took away a good deal of my own devastation.

Later, I had a letter from our spiritual friend Julie, now living in America, telling me that she had seen you in what she called "the golden realm." So, my dear, these reports from clairvoyant friends, revealing that you were in a state of glorious, joyful fulfillment, washed away my sorrow for myself. But there was still a great gap in my life and I longed to know more about your life over there. As you know, through the grace of Swami and some of his clairvoyant children, I did find out some interesting things, which I will give further on in this chapter.

I would like to close this letter with a few phrases from an elegy written after your death by our center's poet and a dear friend of yours, David Whiteman. The whole elegy was published in the "Australian Sai News" soon after your passing.

"I never saw her frown; she always smiled with infectious bliss.
How many others had also been touched by her love?
I watched her week after week; she was always the same.
In silence, I watched her close her eyes and
sing with such joy it lifted my heart.... I often thought,
could I, or any of these attain the wisdom that she had?
Perhaps one day, maybe not in this life. It is a journey and she
knew the final destination.

She looked God in the face and saw the Light,
she became the Light and shone on all she met. To those of
us who have seen the Light, she will always be with us,
just a thought away.......

So with hands in prayer and a smile on my face,
I'll gently say "Om Sai Ram, Iris. I miss your loving hugs,
but you will always be my lovely lady...a devotee from Heaven."

Death may seem to take all away and cut all ties, but it cannot cut the link of the love that is forever. So I can still sign myself your ever-loving husband, Howard.

Highlights from Beyond

After many years of research into what Shakespeare called "the undiscovered country," through such avenues as spiritualism, occult lore and psychic research -- often called parapsychology -- I wrote a book on the subject which is still in circulation under the title, *Beyond Death, the Undiscovered Country.* I fully realized that after all my studies, added to my own personal experience, I had only managed to look into some aspects of a country that still remains largely undiscovered. Large areas still awaited exploration.

Because we don't remember the time we spent there between earth lifetimes, it is perhaps impossible to obtain a full picture. Yet I am always glad to discover new facets of life beyond the veil. So, apart from the joy of finding through communications that Iris was in a state of great happiness -- beyond what it is possible to experience on earth -- I was glad to discover a few new facets of life after death, as well as confirm some I had discovered through my past researches. Perhaps the thing that thrilled me most was to discover a new concept of what we call liberation and merging with the Divine.

The most dramatic and heart-lifting experiences I had in this regard were with the very clairvoyant Sai devotee, Joan Moylan. I consider Joan equal to any clairvoyants we met in the Theosophical Society and, indeed, she seems equal to the great scientist/seer Swedenborg of the eighteenth century. The experience thus gained of Iris' after-life existence was supplemented by two other Sai friends. But I will deal with my sessions with Joan Moylan first.

I have known Joan personally, and by her reputation, for many years. I felt very fortunate when she telephoned to say she was coming to see me a few weeks after the passing of my wife. One sunny morning in the early spring of 1994, she arrived from her home in Queensland. The first thing she said, smiling happily, was, "Iris is coming." "How do you know?" I asked. "I saw her earlier this morning and she told me she was coming." So, in happy expectation, I took Joan to my garden studio which I thought a good place for a quiet session with my beloved, departed wife.

We sat down inside, our chairs facing a big comfortable armchair about two meters away. We hoped Iris would occupy the empty chair. After chatting for about a minute, Joan suddenly said happily, "Iris has just come in and is sitting in the armchair. She looks very beautiful." Joan described her light clothing, her face and hair -- both of which, she said, had the glowing beauty of youth. "How old would you say she looks?" I asked. "Oh, about twenty-seven," she said. This was a big jump back from her seventy-one years at the time of passing, but it confirmed what I had learned in my research on this subject, that deceased people can take on any age in appearance they choose. Very few choose to appear as the old physical body they left behind at death. Yet Paramahansa Yogananda's guru, Yukteswar Giri, was an exception. He came back looking just like the old yogi who had passed away earlier.

Before we had gone far in conversing with Iris, Joan remarked excitedly, "Swami has come into the room and Iris' form has merged with him. He is standing alone by the chair." Then a few moments later she said, "Iris' form has come back out of Swami's form and now they are standing side by side. This is to teach us something." Swami's subtle form moved around the room for a few moments and then disappeared. Iris sat in her chair again and, conversing with her, we understood that this demonstration was to show us that, although merged in God, she had her own form in which to travel to various planes and sub-planes of the other worlds, to do Swami's work. Her work, she explained, was to help people in trouble or distress. "So," I remarked, "you go to them instead of using a telephone as you did here." She replied, "I can go wherever I am required in a flash, but I can also come to earth with the same speed if I feel you need me. But my main work at the present time is in the worlds beyond the earth."

"Do you remember," I asked her, "an interview Swami gave us some time before you left the earth? I asked him if I could reincarnate to help him when he was here as Prema Sai and he said, "Yes, come!" When you asked him the same question, he pointed at you with his finger and said "*Moksha* for you." At first you felt rejected and then realized that you were being given the greatest boon. Do you feel now that you have moksha?" "Yes, I do," she said. "Beyond any doubt, I have moksha." So, I thought to myself, here is a form of liberation, or enlightenment, that combines the two forms described in Buddhism, that is the *ahat,* who remains merged in nirvana, and the *boddhisatva,* who retains his own form to help his brother men. Of course, one must remember that, though forms appear to divide, in reality, they do not.

I had thought from my previous studies that the after-death-state soul remains in the sub-plane to which it goes after death until it has made sufficient progress to move to a higher level. But it seemed that Iris moved where she wished. So I asked her, "In your work, can you move to any plane you wish?" "Yes, I can go to any part that Swami permits," she said. So I said, "In your travels, in your explorations, have you come in contact with any of our loved ones who have passed on?" Her answer showed that she had met many of them, including her own parents, my mother and two sisters but she had not found my father. "I think he must have reincarnated," she said. I hoped he had not because I very much wanted to see him when I went, in due course, to the after-death world. It sounded like a wonderful place, though still mysterious. Picking up my thought, Iris said, "I will take you on a tour of many beautiful areas when you are here, but there will be a good deal of work for you to do up here, Howard." "Oh," I replied, "I will want to rest." "You might at first," she replied, "as I did. But I was so full of bliss and love of God that I wanted to work. I think you will, too. There is much to do for Swami on some of the sub-planes."

We discussed many things during the morning and at one stage we talked about India. I told her I hoped to go there in a few weeks as Swami had invited me to come. She seemed pleased about that and remarked that she would be there, too. "My journey," I said, "will be long and strenuous. You, no doubt, will go in a flash, without the use of airplane."

While we spoke about India, Joan remarked that Iris had changed her attire and was now wearing a beautiful sari of a golden green color. "She changed while she sat in the chair, no doubt," I said, remembering what I had learned in psychic science about manifesting any attire one wishes through the mind and willpower.

"Have you noticed my new photo of Krishna on the wall?" I asked. "Yes," she said, "I'll take a closer look at it." In moving across the studio, she had to pass very close to where Joan was sitting. I was amused to see Joan moving aside, as it were. It was automatic, I expect, because Joan knew even more than I did that Iris' subtle body did not need physical space to move in.

The hours passed too swiftly on this morning of happy reunion and revelation. Joan, who was my instrument in seeing and hearing beyond the veil, seemed to be enjoying herself greatly. When I reminded her that she had an appointment higher up the mountains and had to have lunch before that, she replied, "Oh, I won't bother about lunch. Let's go on talking to Iris." But inevitably the end had to come. As we walked along the garden path back to the house, Joan, who was on my right, said, "Iris is walking on your left." I sensed she was there and put out my arm to encircle her waist, but I felt nothing more than the air. Still it was good to know that she was walking with me again, only a thought away as our poet said. Joan promised that as soon as possible, she would come down from her home in Queensland and we could have another joyous session.

But before the next session with Iris came my visit to Swami in India at Christmas time, 1994. Although he did not say much, his manner revealed that he was sympathetic about my loss of Iris. He praised her in a few words, as he used to do sometimes during her life and he confirmed that she was now with him.

Some weeks later, when Joan arrived for her second party with Iris, she told me that Iris had been standing in the driveway and said, "Welcome, Joan," as she got out of the car. I call it a "party" because this time a number of people came, one of them a being of great spiritual significance.

We went into the studio and Iris came in within a moment or two and sat again on the same chair. I had planned to ask her to inquire if my mother, on the other side, knew anything about the whereabouts of my father. "Perhaps you will ask her, Iris," I said. "Oh," said Iris, "I know already. Your father has reincarnated and is now living in a country in Europe, a small mountainous country. I can't remember its name." But I was to find out a little more before the day was out. I will report here only those things I think will be of interest to the reader.

At some stage, Iris simply vanished from the room. So we sat quietly talking and waiting, hoping she would come back. After a few minutes, she returned and apologized for her sudden departure, explaining that Swami had called her for some urgent job. This took only a few minutes and her actual travel took no time at all.

When we spoke of people on the other side, Iris would ask if I wanted to see them and, if I said yes, they were in the room in a few minutes. One of those who came was my sister, Rita, my childhood playmate, who had died back in 1958. I asked her about her husband, the naval man called Jack. After Rita's passing, Jack's grief had been uncontrollable. When I said he would see her again, he denied violently, even angrily, the statement that there was any life after death. So I wondered if Rita had seen him over there. "Yes," she replied, "I have been to see him a number of times. He is on the third level and doing well."

Another visitor that day was the saintly mother of the O'Brien twins who live in Brisbane and spend much time with Swami. Their mother, Ruth, had died a few weeks before Iris. Joan saw her walking towards our studio through a garden on the other side -- a very beautiful garden, she said. Then Ruth came into the studio and hugged Iris, as was their custom when meeting on earth. Then, in answer to questions, Ruth talked a while about her daughters and her home and garden in Toowoomba in Queensland and said she would like it to be used as a Sai retreat. That and other messages I was able to give to the twins later.

Another important visitor from the other world that day was my sister Leone, whom Swami had said was my twin soul. It seemed rather fitting that she should stand very close to me. "What have you done with our daddy?" I asked, remembering how very close they had been in our family circle. Her reply was, "He has reincarnated into the little country of Liechtenstein in Europe and is now a youth of seventeen years." "I wonder why on earth an ex-farmer from Tasmania should be reborn in that little mountain country," I asked, remembering the beauty of the tiny country when I had driven through it during my years in Europe. I remember also meeting the prince of that country in Germany soon after the war. My sister Leone seemed to know the answer. "He was reborn in a family there who could help him with a problem," she replied. "Also, he believed that he could help them." She, who was once his beloved youngest daughter, seemed to know just what had happened to him and why. I felt again the closeness of our souls as she stood near me in the studio.

But the most remarkable thing that happened that day was after all my visitors had withdrawn except Ruth and Iris. It began with Joan giving a gasp of surprise and leaning forward. At the same time I saw tears falling from her eyes. Her hands were clasped together in a gesture of worship. "What is it, Joan?" I asked. After a while, she answered in a choked voice, "Hanuman is here. He has an arm around each of the two women and his head is touching the ceiling. I feel he is cramming himself down to fit in." The ceiling in my studio is about nine feet high. "Is he doing or saying anything?" I asked. I could feel a divine presence and my own palms went together in prayer as I leaned forward in my chair and almost knelt. "No," Joan replied. "He is just looking at us with a wonderful smile and soft luminous eyes." She tried without much success to describe the beautiful tender expression on his face and the wondrous, seemingly infinite, depths of his eyes. It flashed through my mind that I had on several occasions heard Swami call Hanuman -- who had served the Avatar Rama -- the greatest devotee who ever lived. Why had this supreme devotee of God come to visit us here, I wondered, and why did he have his arms around Ruth O'Brien and my wife? Was he putting his signet of approval on their devotion and service to God? Or was there something else that neither of us understood? All we knew was the great feeling of joy that engulfed us. Then the whole scene in front of us faded into white divine light. Only Hanuman's smiling face remained, shining through the light. Then that, too, vanished and nothing but the light remained. Then the light also went and through the window, we could see the twilight fading into darkness. We had come to the end of a wonderful day in which we had lived in bliss in two worlds. "Shall we ever have more of this?" I wondered aloud. "Yes, we will," said Joan with assurance.

There were others with extrasensory perception who had contacts with Iris after her death. I will give here an experience of two of them. Both were Sai Baba devotees and very reliable witnesses.

Maurice Terragano, who lives in the upper Blue Mountains, is a kabbalist and has a well-developed clairvoyance. He had not known Iris in her lifetime but joined our Lawson center after her death. He came to the *bhajan* singing memorial we held for Iris on the first anniversary of her passing. More than one person saw Iris moving among us in the room full of bhajan singers, but Maurice had the longest and most interesting experience. He saw the separate forms of Swami and Iris and, not knowing her, he thought that she was an angel of Swami. After speaking to him about the bhajans, she left him and merged into Swami's form.

Later he saw her separate again. She went to every individual in the room, he said, and put what looked like a double handful of molten gold into the heart of each individual. There must have been nearly thirty of us.

Another who witnessed the duality of forms with the merging in this kind of moksha was my old friend Elvin Gates. He was in India at Prashanti Nilayam ashram and sitting in *darshan*, having obtained the front row for the first time in weeks, when Swami walked along and paused in front of him. Obtaining permission to touch the Lord's feet, Elvin went onto his knees and did so. Then Swami moved on along the line and, feeling elated by the experience, Elvin sat back in his cross-legged position. Then he felt the light touch of a hand on his shoulder. Looking up, he was surprised and overjoyed to see Iris standing behind him. She looked very beautiful, he told me, and made one of her old familiar remarks that he remembered from when she was on earth. Then, as Swami was getting near the veranda of the *mandir*, she left Elvin and followed him onto the veranda and toward the door of his room. Just before he entered the door, her form merged into Swami's and they went in as one form. "Your story fills me with joy," I said to him, "And it confirms the experiences of other good Sai psychics. I wonder how you felt her subtle hand on your shoulder." "Oh," replied Elvin, who is a very experienced psychic, "Obviously she materialized her hand for the purpose."

I would like to conclude with two lines from a poem written by the English poet, William Johnson Cory, to the Greek philosopher Heraclitus:

> *Still are thy pleasant voices, thy nightingales awake,*
> *For Death he taketh much away, but them he cannot take.*

18

FORGIVENESS, LOVE AND LIBERATION

Start the day with love, spend the day with love, fill the day with love, end the day with love. That is the way to God, for God is Love.

Sathya Sai Baba

"Forgive us our trespasses as we forgive those who trespass against us." These well-known words from the Lord's Prayer have a deeper implication than may at first appear. In his mission on earth, Jesus showed that there was a very close connection between the forgiveness of trespass, or sin, and the healing of diseases. After healing someone, he said such things as "Your sins are forgiven. Now go your way and sin no more." At the healing center of a Christian church I know in Australia, the sick person who seeks healing is told by the Christian minister in charge that before any healing can be accomplished, the patient must ask God for forgiveness. Prior to that he must forgive anyone he thinks has sinned against him. The forgiveness of those who have trespassed against him will, no doubt, involve a search back through the years to unearth anyone against whom he still feels some resentment, a hidden anger or any other signs of non-forgiveness. Having located the person against whom he holds any of these negative emotions, he must declare sincerely in his heart and mind that he truly forgives him. But such a declaration of forgiveness, if he says also in his mind, "But I cannot forget," is not true forgiveness. True forgiveness, effective forgiveness, includes forgetting. Of course, the memory of a wrong he was done may exist somewhere in his mind. It is not as easy as cleaning a word from a slate or erasing it from a piece of paper. Yet if he has forgiven in the deepest sense, he will not think about the memory, or dwell on it. It has lost its former emotional impact. In forgiving those who have trespassed against us, we must effectively forget by never again dwelling on the wrongs we think have been done against us. Until this is accomplished sincerely, we cannot expect the Divine One to forgive our trespasses.

Some patients ask, "Does this mean that God is unable to forgive us until we have truly forgiven all those who have trespassed against us, or is it that he will not?" We must remember that God is omnipotent and can do anything he wills. As well as being omnipotent, he is also omniscient and compassionate; he will answer any prayer that does not go against the ultimate spiritual welfare of the one who prays. Why then the requirement that we must forgive before we are forgiven? And why is the whole process of forgiving and being forgiven essential before truly effective healing of a person's dis-ease?

To understand this, we must take a penetrating look into that which we know as divine, unconditional love. We must be careful not to confuse such love with the so-called romantic love, resulting from Cupid's irresponsible arrow-shooting. That love is an emotional state that keeps a man and woman in a state of constant agitation -- great joy and ecstasy followed by misery and sorrow. Even so, romantic love between man and woman may be an echo of the real thing because it does bring some flashes of the great bliss that lies above the passing joys and pains. Thus, in a sense, it is a promise of the true love that will someday come. Perhaps the best echo in man and other animals of the divine love, for which we are forever searching, is what we call mother love. At its best, it is completely unselfish, giving and forgiving. In its purest state, it demands no return. Yet, like God himself, the mother does enjoy a response of love for love. Mother love is brave, even warrior-like in its protectiveness of its offspring. I have seen mother geese attack big farm horses that have strayed too close to the young goslings. The mother goose will face almost any danger to shield her young from harm. When I was a boy I thought that mother magpies went a bit too far in this. If I inadvertently came too close to a tree where the baby magpies were being hatched out of their shells, I was attacked by mother magpie from the air. Other birds, including plovers, took the same protective, aggressive action against boys whom they thought were likely to steal their eggs. Such love in human beings is equally strong and lasts longer. It can, however, in time become tainted. It may become more attachment than love, sprouting selfish tentacles to contaminate the original selfless love of the mother.

Is it possible, we wonder, to find the pure, selfless never-changing love that forgives and gives and asks nothing in return? Yes, it is possible to find and experience that love. First, let us try to understand what it is. As the great seer-poet Dante said, "Love is the energy that moves the sun and the other stars." In fact, it is the primal power that created the universe and holds it together as one system. It could be called the great cosmic magnet that keeps the wheels of the cosmos turning. As Swami says, God is Love and the energy he emanated in creating the universe -- the primal energy to begin creation and hold it together -- is love.

In Sanskrit, this pure love of God is called *prema* and in the fullness of time this divine magnet, which we call love, draws all things back into conscious oneness with the great Creator. Those who have eyes to see witness its reality around them as the inner truth of the one within the many. Their eyes may fill with tears as their inner vision apprehends this essence of divine oneness in the beauty of a flower or a cloud or the words of a poem. But, above and beyond these occasional flashes of the great truth, there is a way to experience the flow within one's being of this primal prema, or divine love. That is, to come within the aura or the influence of one who is called living divinity, for such a one is a veritable fountain of love. The greatest of these, in my experience, is the living Avatar, Sri Sathya Sai Baba. Undoubtedly there are others on earth today who can, to some degree as Baba does in full measure, open the human heart to release the flow of love that is waiting there. Another heart-opener from my personal experience is the world-travelling saint known as Mata Amritanandamayi. As you come toward her, a powerful beam of pure love embraces you. It is the wonderful influence of Godmen and Godwomen such as these that finds and opens the buried spring of love, pure unconditional love, that is hidden in every person's heart.

But not everyone who has set his feet on the spiritual path will have the good fortune to meet one of these divine surgeons of the spiritual heart who will bring forth the flow of love. Perhaps it is safe to say that the majority will not. Therefore there must be some other way. Yes, there are several. For one, a deep study of the philosophy concerning the reality and truth of divine love is of great help. The following story illustrates that this prema is the primary force within the universe and is the great magnet that holds all in oneness.

This experience is not about the healing of the body through forgiveness and love, but the healing of personal relationships. It took place during the first few months after the end of World War II. I was making a journey by car from my headquarters in the British zone of Germany to Berlin. This meant leaving the British zone at the checkpoint, Helmstedt, and entering the Russian zone. All the exit signs along the autobahn had been changed into Russian script, but I knew the exit that took me off the highway onto the road to a farmhouse of a German family I knew and wished to visit. It was evening when I arrived, and I spent the night expecting to go on to Berlin the next day. But after breakfast, I found two saddled horses tied up not far from the door. The farmer explained that one was for me, the other for one of his daughters who would be my guide. I could not resist the temptation. It was a big farm of some two thousand acres stretching in all directions. It reminded me of my own country. But the German girl did not enjoy her ride. She insisted there was a Russian on horseback following us. I thought she was crazy, but when we returned to the farmhouse, there was a group of some six or seven uniformed Russians waiting there to see us. The upshot was that eventually I was on my way to the office of the

Russian General who was in charge of this whole area of Germany. With me in the car, in addition to my own driver, was a Russian Major from a nearby town and an unshaved Russian soldier carrying a rifle. He, no doubt, was an insurance against my attempt to escape.

On the way, I recalled hearing earlier that two Royal Air Force British Officers had strayed into the Russian zone and had been imprisoned. I had not believed the story, but now I began to wonder if this could happen to me. It seemed inexplicable that our allies in the war could treat us this way. In the big city of Magdeburg, I came to the Headquarters of the General and was led to his office. As I stood in front of his desk, he continued writing and ignored me completely. After a while he looked up with an unfriendly, suspicious expression. There were two German interpreters, one to interpret my English into German, and the other to interpret my German into Russian. Misunderstanding seemed very likely.

The General asked me where I had come from, and I named the town in the British zone where my headquarters were. He stood up and went to the big map that covered the wall behind his desk to find the place where I had started my journey. I saw him looking to the east towards Poland. Somehow, through the chain of interpretation, he must have gotten a wrong message. My impulse was to go behind the desk and show him on the map, but a Russian officer standing near me blocked me from that attempt. The Russian General came and sat down at his desk again, looking at me with more suspicion -- as if he thought I were a spy. What was I doing on a German farm in the Russian zone, he wanted to know. I attempted to explain through the two interpreters, but I could see that he did not believe the story and was more suspicious than ever.

I began to get very angry. I was in a position where he, a Soviet dictator, had all the power. I had heard strange stories. In one, a driver of a Soviet General in Germany had an accident; the General simply drew his pistol and shot the driver dead. This may not have been true, of course, but this General before me now could, if he decided to, have me taken into the bush and shot as a suspected spy. Nobody would know anything about the incident. This thought filled me with maddening rage and fear.

But then a sudden change came. At this time I had not met Sai Baba, but I have proof that he was taking care of me long before we met. It must have been Swami or one of his angels who brought the change to my mind. Suddenly, I felt sorry for the General and his apparent stupidity. Seeing him now as a Russian brother, rather than as a servant of Bolshevik dictatorship, I forgave him completely and sent love from my heart to his heart. It was not difficult to forgive and love a brother of Tolstoy and the other great-souled Russians I had taken into my heart.

A miraculous change came into the officer with my change of heart. The General's eyes became warm and friendly as I apologized for coming into his zone, explaining that I had not known it was forbidden. I said if he would forgive my mistake, I would go straight onto the autobahn and head for Berlin and complete my mission there. This must have touched him because he signed and rubber-stamped a document giving me permission to spend another two hours in the Russian zone before returning to the international highway to Berlin. I had not asked for that, but I was delighted to have time to return to the farm to assure my friends that I was safe, to thank them for their hospitality and to bid them farewell.

The General stood up, clicked his heels and handed me the document with a smile. The faces of the other Russian officers in the General's large office waxed into friendly expressions, and it was as a former ally of Mother Russia that I was escorted from the office back to my car.

In something less that the allotted two hours, I was back on the autobahn headed for the British sector of Berlin. I had learned an important lesson in human relationships.

With this understanding of the mind -- and even with slight glimpses of passing experiences of the divine love in our hearts --

we will do all we can to practice and promote the important power of love in our lives. How do we do that? As the old French bishop said to the young priest on this puzzling question: "You learn to swim by getting in the water and trying until you learn. There are many things you must learn just by doing them and loving is one. You learn to love by loving. The more you practice loving, the more love you will develop, until in the end you will be a master in the art of loving."

That is the key. Realize that it is the most important thing in your life and begin to practice it on your fellow men. Start with those who are easy to love. In the end you will be loving those to whom you are indifferent. Eventually even hate will be replaced by love. Furthermore, this trickle of love for our fellow men can grow into a full stream through heartfelt worship and devotion to one of the princes of love no longer in the body. Two of these are Christ and Krishna. Calling on their hallowed names and picturing their forms will help release the pent-up divine love in the human heart.

Finally, we should be aware that in our own individual, divine plan to love not only all of humanity but all of life, forgiveness is the greatest builder of love. Forgiving others -- and being forgiven by God -- repairs the broken channels through which the unifying and healing streams of love are meant to flow. In the divine business of forgiving, there is one aspect that we should try to understand and remember. You may have heard people say that it is important to forgive ourselves. That is true, but who forgives whom in ourselves? Psychology divides us into many different parts, the number and names depending on the particular system of psychology we study. Divine science divides the human being into two main parts: the lower self, usually called the ego, and the higher Self, synonymous with the God within -- or what the Buddhists call the Center of Enlightenment. These two inhabit one human body.

An interesting analogy is shown in the Indian story of two birds who live in the same tree. One has his nest on the lower branches of the tree. He is a very busy little bird, following his instinctive life of food-gathering, mating and fighting the enemies who want to usurp his territory. Sometimes he is happy, sometimes he is angry and sometimes tragically sad. He catches in his active lifestyle occasional glimpses of another bird living in the thick branches of the tree above him. The bird, with shining plumage, seems to live a very calm and contented life, never fighting with other birds over territory or morsels of food. In fact, though in the same tree, the top bird seems to live in a different world. His songs are not sexual songs to a mate or war songs to an enemy; they are songs of joy flowing from him naturally. In time, the lower bird, by comparison, sees his own little life as a continual struggle on the treadmill of desires. He longs to be like the shining bird -- the calm, beautiful, wise bird on the lofty branches. The wise bird sees all that his little brother on the lower branches is doing. He knows that in the course of time, his brother will learn the vital lessons that will make him discard his agitating desires and start to climb the branches. There he can live the calm, peaceful life of the higher bird, the life of light and joy. The high bird does all he can to help his lower brother upward, until in love they finally merge as one. The busy bird on the lower branches represents the human lower self or ego; the bird in the upper branches symbolizes our higher Self, our true divine Self.

What is known as "forgiving ourselves" must mean that the divine Self -- which has no sins but witnesses the misdemeanors, trespasses and the foolish errors of the thoughtless, desire-filled ego -- must be the forgiver of the sins of the ego. The sinful ego must be forgiven by the divine Self; forgiving ourselves is the same as being forgiven by God. Our inner God is no different from the one great eternal God who is omnipresent in the universe. In brief, to be forgiven by God is the same as forgiving ourselves.

The inner God forgives the erring ego. While the two birds in the story are simply figures in a parable, the Chinese story below reveals a bird with superhuman qualities that are the subject of this Chapter. It is called "The Emperor and the Nightingale" and is said to be based on fact:

A little nightingale used to come and sit on the window sill of the Emperor's bedroom. The bird would sing its immortal song, to the great joy of the Emperor who would fall into a heavenly sleep to the sound of the music. This went on for several months before a rich courtier, who wanted to seek favors of the Emperor, thought of sending him a beautiful, hand-made nightingale with jewelled wings and richly colored plumage. The nightingale was able to sing almost as well as a real nightingale; it rendered its songs whenever the mechanism was turned on. The Emperor was so fascinated that he did not wait for the appearance of the real nightingale.   Rather, every evening he turned on the toy nightingale and listened to its song.

The real nightingale, finding that the Emperor disregarded it and did not need it anymore, ceased to come to the Emperor's window. After a time, however, the Emperor fell ill and gradually got worse. The mechanical bird broke down and nobody in the court could mend it. Through long nights, devoid of music, the Emperor got worse and worse. He longed for his real nightingale to come again. Though it was a humble-looking little bird, its songs were beautiful beyond measure, and it had been faithful to him until he treated it in such a shabby manner.

As the Emperor came near death, his longing to hear his little nightingale grew stronger. Mentally, he beseeched it to forgive him and come again. On one unexpected evening, the miracle took place. The nightingale appeared on the window sill and began his glorious song. It sang its heart out and in the music the Emperor could hear his little friend's forgiveness and love. Every evening without fail, his little feathered friend repeated its wonderful healing song. Soon the Emperor was well again, both in body and mind, for his friend had taught him the lesson of forgiveness.

This story illustrates not only the fact that the one who forgives is healed, but also that healing will come to the one who forgives, for he, too, is brought into a realization of the oneness of all life. God is in all life, Swami teaches, and when our spiritual eye is open, we will see Him there.

The process of forgiving and being forgiven -- mending as it does the shattered truth of oneness -- is one of the most important roads to the state of living in universal love. It is not far from -- and may itself be -- the liberation we seek. It is said that when an individual reaches the state of enlightenment, or liberation from the bondage of all earthly desires, two paths lie open to him. One is that he may rest in nirvana -- which in other words means being merged with the Divine Absolute for eternity. The other way is that through the power of the divine love that is now his very being, he may, while merged in God, help to do the work of God. He may help his brothers and sisters on earth mend the broken bridges that hold them in the sorrows of mortal existence, thus bringing them to the truth and joy he has found. The first way could be called the nirvana of rest and the second the nirvana of divine action. To attempt to describe what this state of nirvana is would be an attempt to describe the indescribable.

Paramahansa Yogananda has given a concept of this that is worthy of our contemplation. He says, in paraphrase, that in time we become tired of everything, even pleasure and happiness. Even from the high heavens of joy, men and gods come back to earth to seek the springboard that will take them beyond the high heavens -- in other words, to unity with God or nirvana. This, he says, is "ever-changing, ever-new, everlasting bliss." That joy, though eternal, is ever new.

The following, I feel, is a worthwhile attempt to explain the inexplicable.

> *When I wake in the morning thy love is there,*
> *Like the golden sunrise in clear mountain air,*
> *And, sheltered all day in thy aura of blue,*
> *I rest in the beauty and love of you.*

Lighting the hours as the day wears through.
Come nearer and nearer, great Lord divine,
Till thy being is mine and mine is thine,
Till this ego can really cease to be,
And I am forever one with thee..
Then, though atoms burst and mountains fall,
No earthly disasters can matter at all,
And even the dark of the cosmic night
Shall shine with thy love in eternal light.

EPILOGUE

In the preceding pages I have tried to present as clearly as possible enlightening experiences -- both outer and inner, my own and those of others -- which I have been blessed to share during my three decades with Sathya Sai Baba and to offer to the reader such understanding as I have gained from them. When I speak of being three decades with Swami, I do not mean I have been continually in his physical presence for all that time. But, as I am now fully aware, from the morning he first smiled at me through an open doorway, he has been ever with me and I with him. The completion of the unification process is the object of whatever earthly years remain to this lifetime. It is, as I have so often said, the goal of all human life though to many it is not yet a conscious goal.

When I complete any book about Sai Baba (this is the fifth), I know how St. John felt when he completed his Gospel about Jesus. I feel that if all the things that have happened to all people whose lives he has touched could be written down in books, they would fill a library larger than any that exists on earth. Deep experiences of Swami's grace and guidance are occurring continually all over the world. I hear of some of them. A few I would like to share with my readers have come to my knowledge since I completed Chapter 18. But I do not want to enlarge this book because eighteen is a good and significant number. Swami points out with approval that eighteen is the number of chapters in the immortal *Bhagavad Gita.* Numerically, it adds up to nine. Nine and its multiples seem to be my *sadguru*'s chosen numbers. While seven was the number of the Old Testament and twelve of the new, nine is the number, in some esoteric way, that belongs to Sathya Sai Baba's testament to mankind. So I am gathering together a small basket of stories whose meaning and significance may deepen in future time. If my allotment of years allows me, I will set them down in a small future book.

Friends have asked me to explain more clearly what effect Sai Baba has had on my life and what changes he has wrought in me.

I had always supposed that such changes were obvious, that I had demonstrated them clearly, if indirectly, by all I have written about him since the late years of the sixties when I first touched an old typewriter in India to write *Sai Baba, Man of Miracles.* But, apparently for many readers, this is not so. With Swami's help, I will try to define these changes.

The changes that have come in my thinking, attitudes, value system and understanding of the meaning and objects of human life -- including my own relationship with people, animals, plant life and all objects of earth; my proper behavior to the whole of my environment; the type of labor, studies, leisure and recreational activities I carry out -- are all an indication of the deep changes that Sai Baba has wrought in me. I must admit, though, that changes in action lag somewhat behind changes in the understanding of true values that Swami molds in the mind and heart. Before God as a man came into my life, my values were self-centered -- selfish rather than selfless. I was ambitious, not so much for money or power, but for fame. I hungered and thirsted, not for rare foods and stimulating beverages, but for new experiences that could be stated as a thirst for an understanding of life. Though I cannot claim to have had a love of all mankind, I had a longing to know mankind in all his variations of race, color and nationality. One of the bosses in my mundane business life simply called this "itchy feet."

What good tendencies one has, Baba amplifies. I have never felt violence or cruelty towards any form of life. As a child, I would weep if I accidentally trod on a spider. When I forced myself to put an earthworm on a hook to go fishing, I inwardly squirmed more than the poor worm. I would play with snakes a long time before I told my father or mother about their presence because I knew that the telling would mean the death of the snake. I hated killing a rabbit or partridge or quail or any other prey of the hunt. But I steeled myself to do such things because hunting and shooting were considered manly sports. I wanted to be as manly as my peers. I did not see then the ugliness of such manliness. My mother was a gentle, saintly soul, so perhaps these beginnings in the ideal of non-violence came from her. However, my innate *ahimsa* (non-violence) was weak and surrendered with little resistance to the examples of violence prevalent among my companions and to the ways of youth in my country life. But after a few years of Swami's influence and teachings, my early dislike of inflicting pain on any kind of animal or insect life grew into a strong repugnance toward violence of any kind -- and with it my compassion for all forms of suffering. I knew, as the Sai spiritual light continued to shine on me, that my tender-heartedness toward my lower brothers in the animal world was not just a weakness, a feminine softness, as most of my male companions considered it to be, but was indeed a high human value that should be practiced by everyone. Sai Baba has led me deeply into the land of non-violence, but he has taught that ahimsa must be practiced with common sense. When someone asked him the question, "What do you do with a mosquito that is about to bite you, Swami?" He replied simply, "Kill it." Swami has said more than once that common sense comes before divine sense.

Perhaps the greatest way in which Sai Baba has changed my life in its attitudes and values, is in leading me to the understanding -- indeed the absolute conviction -- that all life is one with God. This deep-down conviction has made it possible for me to do what previously was not in my disposition and temperament to do. That is, I am now able, without the inner resistance of yore, to extend love to all forms of life everywhere -- even to people I did not like and to some degree still do not like. I tell myself that the dislike is for certain traits of character, whereas the love I send from my heart is to the divine Self, the true Self hidden away in each individual. The love is from God to God, while the love itself is *prema*, or divine love. The link of unity that I feel toward the various species of animals, seems to be a kind of mixture of fatherly and brotherly love. In a sense, this extends at a lower level toward plant life. I find myself talking to plants sometimes and have had proof that they respond. I am not trying to give the impression that I have come to the glorious end of the journey where the highest levels are reached in this divine love, but I am far enough along the journey to feel its effects in my life. The practice of prema becomes easier with time, and meditation and contemplation on the highest manifestations of divine love have shown me that it is the twin sister of that deepest Truth that I have longed to know since my youth and have travelled the world to find. Sai Baba, my Avatar sadguru, has revealed much of that Truth about the meaning of life -- as much as I am, at the present juncture, capable of receiving and understanding.

The effects of this growing light of understanding are a greater, though not yet perfect, peace and a greater calmness within -- which extends outward to my life of action. The Sai *sadhana* (spiritual discipline and practice) has brought insights which have changed, or are changing, my life. As the light of truth, for example, shines into a widening horizon, fears begin to decrease in number. What is considered by many people to be the greatest of all fears -- fear of death -- has completely vanished for me. I feel that I am very fortunate in this and know that all the lesser fears are reluctantly folding up their tents and silently stealing away, as Longfellow puts it. One begins to get a splendid vision of how life, completely without fear, could be.

Many years ago, along the Sai path, I entirely gave up the urge to write for money or fame. I write entirely as a service to Sai Baba, because he has somehow let me know that this is the role I am to play in his great mission. The degree of fame that has come to me through my books I feel sometimes is unwanted and yet brings me the satisfaction that I am not wasting my time. Meantime, I try to ward off the danger of ego expansion.

On the whole, taking an inner view as objectively as possible, I would say that Sai Baba has turned many of my earlier values completely upside down. While I still have a distance to go to reach the ideals of completely selfless motivations and *dharmic,* or righteous, living, the ideals are very clear to me and I strive toward them. The old competitive, selfish pleasures and pastimes of long ago now have no appeal to me whatever. Friends of my worldly days have dropped away. The company I enjoy now is the *satsang* of spiritual people. My most enjoyable leisure is to have some kind friend read me an elevating book. The best is on spiritual subjects, though I do find that some of the literary classics can bring spiritual nourishment and enjoyment.

On the whole, my life has certainly become simplified. Fewer things and simpler things are needed to fill my day with satisfaction. "Don't worry about anything. Just be happy," Swami has often said to me. I strive toward that ideal. I constantly tell myself that *ananda,* or bliss, is one of the basic ingredients of my true Self and that it should shine through my daily life, as do the other two basic ingredients -- consciousness and being. Circumstance should have no effect on the continuity of inner bliss, which we can call happiness. While I am very much aware of this great truth, and strive towards it, I cannot claim to be able to practice it continually. In other words, I am still a *sadhak*, or student, struggling along the spiritual path.

But I can say this: Today, I am very different from the pilgrim whose feet were first led to his star in India in 1965 -- when I could not see it properly through the fog of *maya*. The most significant differences are too subtle to specify and name. So, hoping the reader will find some interest and value in this inadequate sketch, I will conclude this epilogue with a brief dialogue.

I recently told a friend that I had set down for my readers some of the great changes that Swami had brought about in me and in my life. He asked me two questions: "Can you give love? Can you receive love?" When my answer to both questions was in the affirmative, he said, "Well, that's it, then."

GLOSSARY

Advaita:	The philosophy of non-dualism, unity, One-Without-A-Second.
Ahat:	A form of liberation described in Buddhism meaning one who remains merged in nirvana as opposed to a Boddhisatva who retains his own form to help mankind.
Ahimsa:	Nonviolence.
Ananda:	Supreme bliss, unending joy.
Ashram:	Spiritual community.
Atman/atma:	The real Self, one's divinity.
Aum:	The basic primeval sound from which all comes.
Avatar:	An incarnation of God, Descent of God on earth.
Bangaroo:	Golden, a term of affection.
Bhagavad Gita:	The Song of God< major Indian scripture.
Bhajan:	Devotional song of adoration to God.
Bhakti Marga:	Path of devotion.
Bhakti Sutras:	Aphorisms that relate to devotion to God.
Boodhisatva:	Enlightened being who chooses to serve humanity.
Buddhi:	Intellect, innate power of discrimination.
Darshan:	Sight of a holy person.
Dharmic:	Right action, duty, truth, moraltiy, following one's one conscience.
Dhoti:	Indian man's traditional garment.
Guru Marga:	Path of the Guru who leads us to spiritual liberation.
Hatha Yoga:	Postures for physical health.
Jyoti:	Light, flame of a lamp.
Karma:	Activity, action, work. Fate; the consequences of acts done in this life and past lives.
Kosas:	Sheaths.
Kundalini:	Spiritual energy.

Kurukshetra:	Field of action; camp of widked egoistic Kauravas in the *Bhagavad Gita.*
Lingam:	Sacred egg-shaped object; the symbol of Shiva representing the merging of the form with the formless.
Mandir:	Temple.
Mangala sutra:	Marriage necklace.
Manvatara:	A span of time, millions of human life years.
Maya:	The deluding power of the Divine, illusion, ignorance.
Moksha:	Liberation.
Paramaguru:	The most glorious, divine teacher.
Paramatma:	Creator, the Reality, the Supreme Self.
Prana:	Vital breath, vital essence.
Pranava Aum:	The mantra "Aum," the vital vibration that fills the universe.
Prasanthi Nilayam:	Sai Baba's ashram which means "Abode of Peace."
Prasava:	Conception brought about in the ordinary way.
Pravesa:	A virgin birth, not conceived by ordinary means.
Prema:	Divine love.
Puja::	Ritual worship of the Lord.
Puranas:	Ancient sacred books..
Rishis:	Sages.
Sadguru:	Highest teacher, divine teacher.
Sadhak:	Spiritual aspirant.
Sadhana:	Spiritual discipline
Sadhu:	Saint, holy man.
Samsara:	The objective would, sea of change.
Sanathana Dharma:	The ancient wisdom, the eternal path.
Sanskrit:	Ancient Indian language.
Sari:	Indian women's traditional dress.

Satsang:	Good company for spiritual aspirants.
Shaligram:	Symbol of Vishnu in the form of an oval stone.
Shivarathri:	Celebration, literally meaning "the night of Shiva." A time of austerity and intense spiritual practice.
Siva-Shakti:	Male and female aspects of divinity.
Srimad Bhagavata:	Holy book of India.
Trimurti:	The one God may manifest as separate forms such as Brahama, Vishnu and Shiva, but they are only facets of the one Being.
Udivar Gita:	Part of the *Srimad Bhagavata.*
Vedanta:	Philosphy originating in India what teaches the ultimate knowledge, such as "All is One."
Vedas:	Sacred scriptures of the Hindus.
Vibhuti:	Sacred ash.
Yogas:	Disciplines, concentration, self-control. Yoga means union.

Sathya Sai Baba Books from Leela Press

A Catholic Priest Meets Sai Baba by Don Mario Mazzoleni. The theologian discovers through much study and doubt that Sai Baba is a Divine Incarnation. 285 pages, $12.00.

The Dharmic Challenge (Putting Sathya Sai Baba's Teachings into Practice) compiled and edited by Judy Warner. A provocative collection of stories that illustrate the joys and difficulties of living a dharmic life. 181 pages, $11.00.

The Dreams & Realities Face to Face with God by Dr. Naresh Bhatia. The author's devotion to God illuminates the pages of this spiritual autobiography. As head of the blood bank of Sai Baba's Super Specialty Hospital, Bhatia experiences frequent contacts, unique opportunities, and wondrous miracles with Sai Baba. 192 pages, $12.00

Journey to Sathya Sai Baba (A Visitor's Guide) by Valmai Worthington. A primer for first time travelers to Sai Baba's ashram. 86 pages $7.00.

Pathways to God by Jonathan Roof. 27 topics that give a clear and accurate guide to the teachings of Sathya Sai Baba. 211 pages, $12.00.

Sai Baba's Mahavakya on Leadership by Lieut Gen (Retd) Dr. M. L. Chibber. A step-by-step program on how to build character and re-establish leadership inspired by idealism. 212 pages, $12.00.

Sai Inner Views and Insights by Howard Murphet. Another Murphet triumph tracing Murphet's life with Sai Baba over the last 30 years. He not only describes miracles vividly, but shares his experiences and insights into Sai Baba's teachings. 184 pages, $12.00

Song of My Life (A Journey to the Feet of Sathya Sai Baba) by Jeannette Caruth. The author tells the story of her transformation in fluent poetry which occasionally rises to the height of spiritual revelation. 118 pages, $9.00.

Where the Road Ends by Howard Murphet. The author's odyssey in search of the meaning of his life from childhood to old age. The book shows how Baba brings a deeper understanding of life's purpose. 209 pages, $12.00.

If unavailable at your bookstore, call Leela Press (804) 361-1132.